Ethics

WO ES WAR

A series from Verso edited by Slavoj Žižek

Wo es war, soll ich werden – *Where it was, I shall come into being* – is Freud's version of the Enlightenment goal of knowledge that is in itself an act of liberation. Is it still possible to pursue this goal today, in the conditions of late capitalism? If 'it' today is the twin rule of pragmatic-relativist New Sophists and New Age obscurantists, what 'shall come into being' in its place? The premiss of the series is that the explosive combination of Lacanian psychoanalysis and Marxist tradition detonates a dynamic freedom that enables us to question the very presuppositions of the circuit of Capital.

In the same series:

Ethics

An Essay on the Understanding of Evil

ALAIN BADIOU

Translated and introduced by
Peter Hallward

VERSO
London • New York

This book is supported by the French Ministry for Foreign Affairs as part
of the Burgess Programme, headed for the French Embassy in London
by the Institut Français du Royaume Uni

īl institut français

This edition first published by Verso 2001
© Verso 2001
Translation © Peter Hallward 2001
First published as *L'éthique: Essai sur la conscience du Mal*
© Editions Hatier 1993

Paperback edition first published by Verso 2002
© Verso 2002

5 7 9 10 8 6 4

The moral rights of the author and translator have been asserted

Verso
UK: 6 Meard Street, London W1F 0EG
US: 20 Jay Street, Brooklyn, NY 11201

Verso is the imprint of New Left Books

ISBN 978-1-85984-435-9

British Library Cataloguing in Publication Data
A catalogue record for this book is available from the British Library

Library of Congress Cataloging-in-Publication Data
A catalog record for this book is available from the Library of Congress

Typeset in 10/12pt ITC New Baskerville by
SetSystems Ltd, Saffron Walden, Essex
Printed and bound by Cromwell Press Ltd., Trowbridge, Wiltshire

Contents

Translator's Introduction[1]

Intended for a general audience, and first published in a popular series of student-friendly engagements with major philosophical topics (time, art, responsibility, individuality ...), this slender volume provides much the most accessible introduction to Badiou's admittedly complex and unusual thought.

Badiou is no longer a complete stranger among Anglo-American readers. *Ethics* is the third of his books to be translated into English (all within the past year), and his work has already been introduced, summarized and reviewed in a variety of places and ways.[2] There is no need to duplicate such summaries in any detail here. But his work may remain just 'strange' enough to warrant a brief overview of its general orientation, along with some explanation of the precise role played by ethics in his wider conception of things. This conception makes for profitable and provocative comparison with those of his better-known rivals in the field (Lévinas, Derrida ...). I will end this Introduction by asking a couple of the more pressing questions raised by Badiou's intervention in this the most controversial field of contemporary philosophy.

I Badiou's project

Badiou is, by any criteria, one of the most significant and original philosophers working in France today, and perhaps the only serious rival of Deleuze and Derrida for that meaningless but unavoidable title of 'most important contemporary French philosopher'. His attention ranges over a unique combination of fields and commitments: the mathematical theories of sets and categories, modernist poetry and art, radical politics, Lacanian psychoanalysis, contemporary theatre, and the history of philosophy from Plato and Parmenides to Lyotard and Lardreau. He has written more than twenty books, including several successful plays and novels. He edits the prestigious collection 'L'Ordre Philosophique' at Les Editions du Seuil, and is a professor at the Ecole Normale Supérieure in Paris and at the Collège International de Philosophie, where his lectures consistently draw hundreds of listeners.

Broadly speaking, Badiou's philosophy seeks to expose and make sense of the potential for radical innovation (revolution, invention, transfiguration . . .) in every situation. Simplifying things considerably, we might say that he divides the sphere of human action into two overlapping but sharply differentiated sub-spheres: (a) the 'ordinary' realm of established interests and differences, of approved *knowledges* that serve to name, recognize and *place* consolidated identities; and (b) an 'exceptional' realm of singular innovations or *truths*, which persist only through the militant proclamation of those rare individuals who constitute themselves *as the subjects* of a truth, as the 'militants' of their cause.

The realm of knowledge is essentially static, 'objective', and structured according to the interests of those who dominate and govern the situation; every ordinary situation is 'structured in dominance', as Althusser would say. The sum total of these structurings – namings, classifications, divisions, distributions – make up what Badiou calls the *state* of the situation. (Badiou's use of the term 'state' incorporates a classically Marxist understanding of the political state as much as it overlaps with a simple intuitive understanding of the 'status quo'.) In an ordinary situation, the domination of its state is effectively absolute – indeed, so absolute as to be beyond any precise measurement or determination. It is precisely this indetermination that ensures conformity or obedience from the (classified, divided . . .) members of the situation.

Access to the realm of truth, by contrast, is achieved through a procedure that succeeds both in *fixing* the domination of the state over the situation and in *evading* this domination. This procedure is wholly subjective: it is founded only on the subjects who 'bear' its trajectory. A truth proceeds as a 'subtraction' from the particularity of the known (from the classifications of the state). A truth is innovation *en acte*, singular in its location and occasion, but universal in its 'address' and import. Inaccessible to the classifications of the state, the truth comes to pass as a universal-singular, particular to but unlimited by the contents of the situation in which it comes to exist.

Such a truth-procedure can begin only with some sort of break with the ordinary situation in which it takes place – what Badiou calls an *event*. An event has no objective or verifiable content. Its 'happening' cannot be proved, only affirmed and proclaimed. Event, subject, and truth are thus all aspects of a single process of affirmation: a truth comes into being through those subjects who maintain a resilient *fidelity* to the consequences of an event that took place *in* a situation but was not *of* it. Fidelity, the commitment to a truth, amounts to something like a disinterested enthusiasm, absorption in a compelling task or cause, a sense of elation, of being caught up in something that transcends all petty, private or material concerns. Subjects are both *carried by* a truth – they compose the 'finite' points of an always 'infinite' truth – and provide its literal, material 'support'. Every subject *is* only an 'objective' individual, an ordinary mortal, become 'immortal' through his or her affirmation of (or transfiguration by) a truth that coheres at a level entirely beyond this mortal objectivity.

Truth for Badiou thus evokes the logic of *being true* to something, of *holding true* to a principle, person, or ideal. His examples include, in characteristically diverse registers: Saint Paul's militant conception of an apostolic subjectivity that exists only through proclamation of an event (the resurrection of Christ) of universal import but of no 'objective' or established significance; the Jacobin or Bolshevik fidelity to a Revolutionary event which exceeds, in its subjective power and generic scope, the particular actions that contributed to its occurrence; two lovers' conception of themselves as amorous subjects, 'rooted' only in a fidelity to the ephemeral event of their encounter; an artist's or scientist's fidelity to a creative line of inquiry opened up by a discovery or break with tradition. . . . In each case, what is materially composed by such truth-procedures is a 'generic set' to which only the most disinterested (most universal, most anonymous) 'stuff' of the situation belongs.

The eclectic range of Badiou's illustrations is balanced by

their rigorous distribution among four and only four fields of truth (each of which defines one of the four 'conditions' of philosophy, or 'generic procedures'): love, art, science, and politics. Why these particular four? Because they mark out the possible instances of the *subject* as variously individual or collective. Love, clearly, affects only the individuals concerned. Politics, by contrast, concerns only the collective dimension, the affirmation of an absolutely generic equality. And in 'mixed situations' – situations with an individual 'vehicle' but a collective import – art and science qualify as generic to the degree that they effect a pure invention or discovery beyond the mere transmission of recognized knowledges.[3]

II Why 'ethics'?

The part played by 'ethics' in this configuration is an essentially regulative one. Understood in terms of a philosophy of truth, 'ethical' should simply describe what helps to preserve or en-*courage* a subjective fidelity as such. The ethical prescription can be summarized by the single imperative: 'Keep going!' or 'Continue!' For a truth is clearly difficult by definition. It implies an effectively *selfless* devotion to a cause. By going against the current, by going against the 'natural' movement of time itself, it is vulnerable to various forms of erosion at every moment of its elaboration. To *keep going*, then, presumes the ability to identify and resist the various forms of corruption or exhaustion that can beset a fidelity to truth.

This corruption defines what Badiou calls 'Evil' [*le Mal*]. Evil can take one of three main forms, each one a perversion of truth: (a) betrayal, the renunciation of a difficult fidelity; (b) delusion, the confusion of a mere 'simulacrum' of an event with a genuine event; and (c) terror, or the effort to impose the total and unqualified power of a truth. The first perversion is a fairly straightforward matter of temptation and fatigue. The second involves confusion of the necessarily universal address of every genuine event (ensured, in a somewhat technical sense, by its location at the edge of the 'void' of the situation in which it takes place)[4] with a particular, differentiating address, one located in the substantial '*plenitude*' of a certain community, people or place: the example that Badiou develops in some detail, here, is Nazism. The third perversion evokes the conventionally tragic realm of hubris: in order to 'keep going', the subject of truth must resist the temptation to impose an absolute, definitive order of truth (or, as Badiou will say: to 'force' its 'unnameable' limit). Such an imposition would effectively 'objectify the truth', resulting in a fatal confusion of the two realms distinguished at every stage of Badiou's philosophy (objective knowledge and subjective truth). Badiou's examples include positivism, Stalinism and the latter stages of China's Cultural Revolution. In short: 'Simulacrum (associated with the event), betrayal (associated with the fidelity), and the forcing of the unnameable (associated with the power of the true): these are the figures of Evil, an Evil which becomes an *actual* possibility only thanks to the sole Good we recognize – a truth-process.'[5]

An ethic of truths, then, is designed to cultivate: a sense of discernment (do not confuse the true and the false); courage and endurance (do not betray the true); moderation and restraint (resist the idea of total or 'substantial' truth).

The logic relation of Good and Evil is thus perfectly clear:

first the Good (the affirmation of a truth), *then* the risk of Evil (as perversion of the Good). The polemic thrust of the book's opening chapter follows as an equally logical consequence, for the recent liberal-humanist recourse to ethics – what Badiou calls our 'ethical ideology' – presumes the opposite derivation: first the assumption of an a priori evil (totalitarianism, violence, suffering), then the imposition of an essentially defensive ethics, a 'respect' for negative liberties and 'human rights'. 'Ethics' here simply means protection from abusive interference. It amounts to an intellectual justification of the status quo. Operating exclusively in the realm of consensus, of the 'self-evident', ethics is intrinsically conservative.

The prevailing 'ethical ideology' has two 'philosophical' poles. First, a (vaguely Kantian) universalizing pole which, indifferent to the particularity of any given situation, proscribes in advance any possibility of an organized, militant and *situated* intervention in the name of some collective 'Good': ethics here is grounded in the abstract universality of general 'human' attributes or rights. And second, a (vaguely Lévinasian) differential pole, attuned to the irreducible alterity of the Other: ethics here is expressed in an equally abstract respect for mainly cultural 'differences'. Neither *this* universality nor *this* alterity, Badiou suggests, can be rigorously founded without tacit reference to theology. Either way, the ethical ideology conceives of 'man' as a fundamentally passive, fragile and *mortal* entity – as a potential victim to be protected (most often, as a 'marginalized', 'excluded' or 'Third World' victim, to be protected by a dutiful, efficient, and invariably 'Western' benefactor/exploiter).

By contrast, an ethic of truths presumes that every

individual can be active and 'immortal', is indifferent to
established or state-sanctioned differences, operates in the
realm of practical division (for or against the event), and
situates its affirmation precisely there where the state of the
situation can see only the non-known and the non-obvious.

Badiou's fundamentally 'divisive' ethics makes no less of
a claim to universality than does its ideological rival. Simply,
its universality is a rigorously situated *project* in something
like the Sartrean sense: it persists as an unending compilation of what, in the situation, is addressed 'for all', regardless of interest or privilege, regardless of state-sanctioned
distinctions (and thus against those who continue to defend
those privileges and distinctions). A truth compiles, step by
step, everything that affirms the strictly generic universality
of all members of the situation. The point is that any such
generic affirmation cannot be made 'in theory' or a priori,
as the basis for an established consensus. It can take place
only through an 'evental [*événementiel*]' break with the status
quo, a break sparked by an event that eludes classification
in the situation. And it can continue only through a fidelity
guarded against its Evil distortion. 'The' ethic of truth,
then, is fully subordinate to the particularity of *a* truth.
There can be no 'ethics in general', no general principle of
human rights, for the simple reason that what is *universally*
human is always rooted in particular truths, particular configurations of active thought.

The combination of trenchant polemic and exuberant
affirmation makes *Ethics* the closest thing Badiou has written
to a manifesto (even more, I think, than the book entitled
Manifesto for Philosophy). The polemic is directed, first and
foremost, against the so-called '*nouveaux philosophes*' –
against André Glucksmann in particular, along with other

well-known critics of *la pensée '68* (Alain Renaut and Luc
Ferry, among others). His argument extends, however, to a
(generally implicit) confrontation with positions as diverse
as those of Rawls, Habermas, Benhabib, Ricoeur, Rorty,
Irigaray, and much of what is called 'cultural studies' in
North America. Against these varieties of more or less
respectful humanism, Badiou takes up and defends the
variously antihumanist *and* progressive positions of Foucault, Althusser and Lacan. He rejects the almost universally
accepted argument that ethics should essentially concern
the Other as such (as potential victim of violence or misre-
cognition). In what will probably be the most startling
sentence of the book for many Anglo-American readers, he
insists: 'All ethical predication based on recognition of the
other should be purely and simply abandoned.' Why?
Because the real practical and philosophical question concerns the status of the *Same*. Differences being simply *what
there is*,[6] the question of what 'ought to be' must concern
only what is valid for all, at a level of legitimacy that is
indifferent to differences. Differences *are*; the Same is what
may *come to be* through the disciplined adherence to a
universal truth. For a truth is not founded on some privileged part of the situation, on the basis of some particular
class or community of people; rather, its 'site' is determined
by proximity to what is most vulnerable, most anonymous
in the situation (i.e. what is perceived as empty or *void* from
the perspective adopted by those who dominate the situation).[7] Collective privileges or differences are precisely
what any truth, in its coming to be, deposes or renders
insignificant. Every truth, every compiling of the Same, is
subtracted from, or transcends, the merely known or established, the merely differ-ed.

The properly ethical question, again, emerges at that supremely dangerous point where this generic Same might deteriorate into an Evil uniformity or chauvinism. It is always Evil to justify (as opposed to a truth 'founded' only on what is most empty of substance, i.e. on the *void* of the situation) the assertion of substantial or communal conformity, and with it to justify the aggressive liquidation of difference (as opposed to a reserved indifference to differences). Against this an ethic of truths deploys its principles of courage, discernment and reserve. In the end, Badiou's conception is very simple: Ethics is what helps a truth (a compilation of the same-through-subtraction) to persist.

III Lacan and Kant

The major and immediate inspiration for Badiou's ethics is his 'master' Jacques Lacan. Lacan's search for *an* ethics of psychoanalysis provides Badiou with the model for a procedure-specific approach, and Lacan's famous imperative 'do not give up on your desire [*ne pas céder sur son désir*],'[8] furnishes him with an abstract principle valid for every such procedure. For to be thus faithful to the peculiarity of your desire first requires 'a radical repudiation of a certain idea of the good',[9] that is, the repudiation of all merely *consensual* social norms (happiness, pleasure, health . . .) in favour of an exceptional affirmation whose 'value' cannot necessarily be proved or communicated. Examples from the Lacanian pantheon include Antigone in her cave, Oedipus in his pursuit of the truth, Socrates condemned to the hemlock, Thomas More in his fidelity to Catholicism, Geronimo in his refusal to yield to an inevi-

table defeat. . . .[10] Desire cares no more for the approval of
others than for our own happiness. Rather, the ethical
question 'is to be articulated from the point of view of the
location of man in relation to the *Real* [*réel*]',[11] that is to say,
the traumatic, irreducible, essentially asocial and asymbolic
particularity of *your* experience. Since your 'normal' conscious life (your psychological 'status quo') is structured
around the repression of this Real, access to it must be
achieved through an 'essential encounter'[12] (i.e. what
Badiou will call an *event*, a happening which escapes all
structuring 'normality'). Ethics is what helps the subject to
endure this encounter, and its consequences. Thus guided
by an ethics of the Real, analysis can lead, with time, to 'the
advent of a *true* speech and the realization by the subject of
his history'.[13] (Beckett's stubborn persistence – 'I can't go
on, I will go on' – is, for Badiou, exemplary of such a *real*
ization.)[14]

What distinguishes Badiou's *philosophical* ethics from
Lacan's own essentially '*anti-philosophical*' stance is the precise status allocated to the Real in this arrangement.[15]
Badiou emphasizes the topological location of the Real,
the Real as 'being, in a situation, in any given symbolic
field, the point of impasse, or the point of impossibility,
which precisely allows us to think the situation as a
whole'.[16] The Real is what seems empty or void from the
perspective of those who re-present and dominate the situation (i.e. from the perspective assumed by the 'state of
the situation'); rejected from any stable assignation of
place, it is thereby that which calls into question the prevailing regime of place and placement *tout court*.[17] Badiou's
Real is always strictly situation-specific. But from a later
Lacanian perspective, the unsymbolizable Real often comes

to indicate general human finitude in its most elementary form, that is, death. As Lacan's most forceful contemporary disciple puts it:

> The whole of Lacan's effort is precisely focused on those limit-experiences in which the subject finds himself confronted with the death drive at its purest, prior to its reversal into sublimation. . . . What 'Death' stands for at its most radical is not merely the passing of earthly life, but the 'night of the world', the self-withdrawal, the absolute contradiction of subjectivity, the severing of its links with 'reality'.[18]

A Lacanian ethics is designed to enable us to endure this severing without flinching, as the price to be paid for a 'symbolic New Beginning, the emergence of the "New Harmony" sustained by a newly emerged Master-Signifier'. And it is at this point, Žižek continues, that 'Lacan parts company with Badiou' (154). For confrontation with Lacan's Real here amounts to an experience of the abject, inarticulable realm of the *corpse* as such – the 'undead' that is Oedipus after his mutilation, or Antigone reduced to her 'living death'.[19] Žižek accepts this reduction without hesitation. Since 'modern subjectivity emerges when the subject perceives himself as "out of joint", as excluded from the order of things, from the positive order of entities', so 'for that reason, the ontic equivalent of the modern subject is inherently excremental. . . . There is no subjectivity without the reduction of the subject's positive-substantial being to a disposable "piece of shit"' (157). From Žižek's perspective, what thus 'remains beyond Badiou's reach . . . is this domain "beyond the Good", in which a human being encounters the death drive as the utmost limit of human experience, and pays the price by undergoing a radical "subjective destitution", by being reduced to an excremental remainder' (161).

Badiou would no doubt plead guilty as charged. For the great virtue of his system, compared with Lacan's, is surely its *separation* of the merely ineffable, in-significant horror of death from the generic 'destitution' or subtraction no doubt demanded by every subjectification. It is Badiou's achievement to have subtracted the operation of truth from any redemption of the abject, and to have made the distinction between living and unliving, between finite and infinite, a matter of absolute *indifference*. The 'Real' emergence of 'the undead-indestructible object, [of] Life deprived of support in the symbolic order'[20] is incapable of provoking the slightest reaction either from within the domain of purely multiple being-as-being on the one hand, or from the domain of an infinite, properly *immortal* subjectivization on the other. From Badiou's perspective, death can never qualify as an event.

A second and no less inviting point of comparison is provided by one of the explicit targets of Badiou's own critique, Immanuel Kant – a thinker whose influence on Lacan's own ethics is well known.[21] Like Badiou, Kant abstracts questions of ethics from all 'sensibility',[22] and also like Badiou, he posits the universal as the sole legitimate basis for subjective action, through the familiar command to 'act on a maxim that at the same time contains in itself its own universal validity for every rational being' (438). It was Kant who first evacuated the ethical command of any substantial content, so as to ground ethical 'fidelity' in nothing other than the subject's own *prescription*. 'The unique strength of Kant's ethics,' as Žižek explains,

> lies in this very formal indeterminacy: moral Law does not tell me *what* my duty is, it merely tells me *that* I should accomplish my duty. That is to say, it is not possible to derive the concrete norms I have to follow in my specific situation from the moral Law itself – which means that the subject himself has to assume the responsibility of 'translating' the abstract injunction of the moral Law into a series of concrete obligations. . . . The only guarantor of the universality of positive moral norms is the subject's own contingent act of performatively assuming these norms.[23]

Kant's very procedure – the evacuation of all heteronomous interests and motives, the suspension of all references to 'psychology' and 'utility',[24] all allusion to any 'special property of human nature' (425), all calculation required to obtain 'happiness' or 'welfare' (394) – bears some resemblance to Badiou's. What remains paramount for both is a specifically *subjective* (and explicitly 'infinite') power. When Kant says: 'I ought never to act except in such a way that I could also will that my maxim should become a universal law' (402), the active *willing* is an essential component of the criterion (424). Moreover, Badiou is no less incapable than Kant of providing an 'objective' explanation of the noumenal basis of this subjective capacity (i.e. a definition or *description* of what the subjective axiom prescribes). We might say that from the Kantian perspective, ethics must accept as its own *unnameable* 'the subjective impossibility of *explaining* the freedom of the will' (459–60).

However significant this *rapprochement* might seem, what

sets Badiou's ethics clearly apart from Kant's categorical imperative is his unwavering insistence on the particular and exceptional character of every ethical obligation. What Badiou objects to in Kant is not, of course, the association of truth with an infinite reality 'independent of animality and the whole world of sense', but, rather, the association of this reality with a transcendental *normality*. Kant grounds the authority of *the* moral law in the *fact* of freedom and the faculty of reason.[25] Having banished the transcendent One from his ontology, Kant restores it in his morality.[26] Badiou, by contrast, argues that only ontological infinity is 'normal'; every subjective (i.e. ethical) infinity is an exception to the rules, including moral rules. Badiou's ethics is *essentially* incommensurable with the whole Kantian register of legality, duty, obligation, and conformity. Nothing is less consistent with Badiou than a prescription to act 'for the sake of the law' as such,[27] and nothing is more foreign to his notion of the subject than the idea of a will governed by purely a priori principles.

IV Abandoning the ethics of Otherness

Building on these foundations – a *topological* understanding of the situation (adapted from Lacan) and a *universalist* understanding of prescription (adapted from Kant), reinforced with a rigorously *infinite* understanding of subjective 'freedom' (adapted from Cantor as much as from Sartre) and a *strategic* appreciation of historical opportunity or *conjoncture* (adapted from Althusser as much as Lenin) – Badiou has devised an ethics so fundamentally at odds with the view that generally prevails in the Anglo-American academy as to be almost unreadable. This 'prevailing view', adapted from quite different sources (Lévinas, Derrida, Irigaray, and Spivak are among the most frequently cited names), is organized, of course, around the category of the *other*. Perhaps nothing is more orthodox today than a generalized reverence for the other *qua* other. Before going any further, and at the risk of considerable simplification, it may be worth briefly outlining what is at stake in this impending controversy, which may well turn out to be one of the most telling in contemporary philosophy.

For Badiou, true ethical questions can arise only in a specific situation and under circumstances which, however *divisive*, are essentially *indifferent to differences*, concerning subjects 'disinterested' in the other as such, the other *qua other* (i.e. in the circumstances created by a truth-procedure). The 'ethical ideology', by contrast, precisely presumes to transcend all situated restrictions and to prevail in a consensual realm beyond division, all the while orientated around the imperious demands of difference and *otherness qua otherness*, the difference of the *altogether* other as much as the irreducibly incommensurable demands of *every* particular other. As Badiou is the first to recognize, nowhere is the essential logic more clearly articulated than in Lévinas's philosophy, where 'the Other comes to us not only out of context but also without mediation. . . .'[28] According to Lévinas, there can be no ethical *situation* as such, since ethics bears witness to a properly meta- or pre-ontological responsibility (roughly, the responsibility of a creature to its transcendent creator, a creator altogether beyond the ontological field of creation). For Lévinas, as for Derrida after him, the other is *other* only if he immediately evokes or expresses the *absolutely* (divinely) other.

Since the alterity of the other is simultaneously 'the alterity of the human other [*Autrui*] and of the Most High [*Très Haut*]',[29] so then our responsibility to this other is a matter of 'unconditional obedience', 'trauma', 'obsession', 'persecution', and so on.[30] Of course, the limited creatures that we are can apprehend the Altogether-Other only if this otherness appears in some sense 'on our own level', that is, in the appearing of our 'neighbour' (of our neighbour's *face*): there is only 'responsibility and a Self because the trace of the [divinely] Infinite ... is inscribed in proximity'.[31] But this inscribing in nearness in no sense dilutes the essential fact that in my 'non-relation' with the Other, 'the Other remains absolute and absolves itself from the relation which it enters into'.[32] The relation with the other is first and foremost a 'relation' with the transcendent beyond as such. Lévinasian ethics, in short, is a form of what Badiou criticizes as *anti*-philosophy, that is, the reservation of pure or absolute value to a realm beyond all conceptual distinction.

Although Derrida's less overtly theological thematics invite more interesting comparisons with Badiou (thanks, for instance, to his *comparable* emphasis on the exceptional singularity of the ethical subject, on the radical novelty of what is 'to come', on the necessity of a decision that remains inaccessible to knowledge or proof...),[33] his recent explorations of ethical responsibility conform, in the last analysis, to a similarly anti-philosophical orientation. Couched most notably in terms of the logic of the *gift*, Derrida's ethical reflections circle obsessively around notions of inaccessibility and secrecy, around that which is beyond presentation or identification, around subjective 'impossibility', around 'madness' and 'forgetting', and so on.[34] Following on from

Lévinas, Derrida says that I am responsible to the other, I am called to obey the call of the other (moreover, of *every* other), simply because the other (every other) is indeed *other*, absolutely other: '*Tout autre est tout autre.*'[35] This formula ensures a quasi-redemptive confusion of 'each' or 'every' other with the 'Altogether-Other', or God.[36] 'God, as the wholly other, is to be found everywhere there is something of the wholly other. And since each of us, everyone else, each other is infinitely other in its absolute singularity, inaccessible, solitary, transcendent, nonmanifest,' so then 'my relation without relation to every other as altogether other [*tout autre comme tout autre*]' (76/78tm) is of essentially the same order as my relation to God – or, indeed, to *myself.* To 'myself', since what God *is* is 'simply' that configuration of secrecy which preserves absolute alterity as such, be it the alterity within me (in so far as *I* never coincide with what can be known of my 'ego') or beyond me, in others (in so far as they, too, never coincide with their *persona*, or public role).[37] Whether God is thus to be 'situated' in our apparently private 'structure of conscience' or, rather, invested in a fully transcendent 'beyond', ceases to be a pertinent question. *What matters, either way, is the logic of secrecy as such*, a solitary secrecy that is both private and transcendent. What matters is that 'God looks at me and I don't see him and it is on the basis of this gaze that singles me out [*ce regard qui me regarde*] that my responsibility comes into being' (87/91). What matters is that we obey God, who is 'himself absent, hidden and silent'; what matters is that 'the other as absolute other, namely, God, must remain transcendent, hidden, secret' – failing which, of course, 'he wouldn't be God, we wouldn't be dealing with the Other as God or with God as wholly other' (59/57, 67/67). What matters above all is secrecy itself: 'secrecy [*le secret*] is essential to the exercise of this absolute responsibility' (67/ 67). Derrida's secret God, whether vested in the exteriority of the other or drawn from the invisible interiority of the self, fits comfortably within Badiou's definition of religion as the endless effort to sustain a questioning confrontation with the 'inaccessible', 'inscrutable' or 'impenetrable'.[38]

Like Badiou, Derrida is careful to distinguish the realm of decision from the realm of knowledge. To reduce my decision to respond to the calculus of reasons and the assessment of possibilities is to eliminate its radical character as a *decision*. The decision must always concern what I cannot *know*. Ethics is a matter of 'responsibility in the experience of absolute decisions made outside of knowledge or given norms'.[39] But Derrida does not stop there. The responsible decision must concern not only the not-known, it must evade conceptualization altogether. 'In order for [absolute responsibility] to be what it must be it must remain inconceivable, indeed unthinkable.'[40] The decision becomes precisely what is impossible for the *subject* as such. If, then, a response or a decision does take place, it can only have been 'the decision of the other in me'.[41] Like Abraham responding to God's instruction to sacrifice his son, I must respond without trying to interpret (and thus appropriate) the other's meaning. I must respond simply because radical otherness demands it; only then do I become the unknowing vehicle for this other's decision. Hence the *mysterium tremendum* whose 'trembling' quivers throughout *Donner la mort*: 'we fear and tremble before the inaccessible secret of a God who decides for us although we remain responsible'.[42] Hence, too, the irreducibly 'tragic' and 'guilty' quality of Derrida's ethical responsibility

(54–5/51), the impasse of a responsibility to impossibly overwhelming (and impossibly incommensurable) obligations. This impasse, moreover, is only exacerbated by any attempt to *justify* an ethical decision. Since every such decision must be made by a fully solitary or 'irreplaceable' subject, so then its justification according to the necessarily general or universal criteria of collective ethics threatens 'to dissolve my singularity in the medium of the concept', to betray my secret within the publicity of language – in short, to threaten me with replacement.[43] If it is to be a genuine decision, it seems, the decision must take place as a pure leap of faith, one that resists any location in the situation, any justification by its subject, and any 'conceptualization' by philosophy.

Badiou's emphasis on the material topology of a truth-procedure, by contrast, is designed precisely to situate every such leap and to justify every apparently 'unjustifiable' commitment in terms of its eternal and universal address. The decision is no less 'incalculable', no less extra-ordinary or extra-legal. But for Badiou, an ordinary (replaceable) individual *becomes irreplaceable, becomes a (singular) subject,* only through this very commitment itself; it is only the commitment to a truth-process that '*induces* a subject'.[44] Whereas Derrida maintains that responsibility to 'the absolute singularity of the other . . . calls for a betrayal of everything that manifests itself within the order of universal generality',[45] Badiou declares that we can access the realm of singularity only through adherence to strictly universal criteria – that is, to the universality produced by *a* truth-procedure. Derrida's responsibility keeps itself 'apart and secret', it 'holds to what is apart and secret' (33/26tm); whereas Badiou's commitment, inspired by Lacan's logic of the *matheme* – the *literal* basis for an 'integral transmission' of truth[46] – pursues clarity for all. Derrida's tension between (singular) subject and (collective) justification disappears here without trace, as does every hint of pathos roused by a responsibility deemed impossible a priori. A *true* statement, as Badiou conceives it, is precisely one that can be made by *anyone,* anyone at all.[47] Again, with Badiou, impossibility is invariably thought in terms of a particular situation, that is, as the *Real* of that situation, the void around which it is structured in its systematic entirety – and thus the point from which, through a process of eminently '*logical* revolt',[48] it becomes possible to transform the situation as a whole. And whereas both Badiou and Derrida orientate their ethics around the advent of something 'to come' that escapes incorporation within any logic of anticipation or figuration, Badiou's event remains *situated vis-à-vis* the state of the situation (the elements of the 'symptomal' or 'evental' site [*site événementiel*] are perfectly accessible 'in their own right'; they are inaccessible only from within the perspective adopted by the *state* of the situation), whereas Derrida's messianic event is *simply* 'monstrous' in the strong sense, consigned to a general 'formlessness'.[49]

What Irigaray and Spivak – to mention only two of many further voices in the varied but harmonious ethical chorus – contribute to this scheme is a more 'embodied' quality, a more 'substantially' othered understanding of otherness. The contrast with Badiou's orientation becomes proportionally more emphatic. As a rule, the more specified the content of what Deleuze once criticized as the 'Other structure',[50] the more vehemently Badiou denounces it.

We might say that with Irigaray, Derrida's *monster* is given a specific sexual location – call it 'mucosity' for short, the 'ecstatic' indistinction achieved through penetration into 'the mucous membranes of the body'.[51] Whereas Badiou's subject, through fidelity to an event in love, seeks to subtract a *truth* of sexual difference from all positive or culturally validated indicators (i.e. from what can be *known* of sexual difference), Irigaray's goal is precisely 'social and cultural sexualization for the two sexes'.[52] This effort leads her to assert 'women's right to their own specific culture',[53] complete with a specifically feminine 'sort of social organization, ... a religion, a language, and either a currency of their own or a non-market economy'.[54] Where Badiou pursues the extra-legal or illegal solidarity of a universal truth, Irigaray calls for 'laws that valorize difference'.[55] Where Badiou seeks to free 'generic humanity' from the manipulations of the state, Irigaray seeks to reinforce official classifications of sex, culminating in 'the legal encodification of virginity (or physical and moral integrity) as a component of female identity'.[56] And whereas Badiou seeks a precise and systematic conceptual description (in love and sexual difference as in everything else), Irigaray embraces a typically anti-philosophical distrust of concepts and a deliberately anti-systematic means of presentation.[57] Not only, then, does Irigaray look forward to the day when 'the mutual obligations of mothers-children shall be defined by civil law',[58] she seeks to renew the *essentially* obscure 'bond of female ancestries',[59] to restore a lost era of 'woman's law', a time when 'the divine and the human were not separate'.[60] There can be few better illustrations of the 'ethical' logic Badiou so firmly opposes: reliance upon a legislative or state-brokered mechanism with a communitarian or essentialist (indeed, expressly *inegalitarian*) twist.[61]

Space allows for only one further (and no less brutally

simplified) point of comparison: with one aspect of the recent work of Gayatri Chakravorty Spivak. Broadly in line with 'Derrida's work on the ethical, on justice and the gift', Spivak's approach is increasingly orientated towards 'the singular and unverifiable margin' that both discloses and refracts the (non-?)presence of the 'wholly other'.[62] Pushing her readers to 'acknowledge a responsibility toward the trace of the other', Spivak seeks to confront, in her bearing-witness to those she famously names the 'subaltern' (roughly, those marginalized or exploited to a degree beyond any dialectical 'integration'), 'an unascertainable ethical singularity that is not ever a sustainable condition'.[63] In her own 'non-relation' with the subaltern, this implies an effort to 'establish an ethical singularity with the woman in question ... the impossible project of ethical singularity, woman-on-woman, is the only way we teach, and learn'.[64] Impossibility is again to be taken in an ultimately non-situational sense ('no amount of raised-consciousness field-work can even approach the painstaking labour to establish ethical singularity with the subaltern').[65] And as is typical of our 'ethical ideology', the upshot is an effectively a priori condemnation of disciplined political intervention. 'Most political movements fail in the long run,' Spivak tells us, 'because of the absence of this [ethical] engagement. In fact, it is impossible for all leaders (subaltern or otherwise) to engage every subaltern in this way, especially across the gender divide. This is why ethics is the experience of the impossible' (270). Any organized political engagement in these circumstances must indeed appear 'contradictory and aporetic'.[66] We are left simply with the vague *spectacle* of 'an impossible social justice glimpsed through remote and secret encounters with singular figures'.[67]

This is a conclusion that Badiou seeks to avoid at all costs, without evading the *precise* philosophical implications of (always historical) singularity and (always situational) impossibility. Whereas the deconstructive project is determined to fold every emergence of the new back into a structure of iterability and repetition ('every declared rupture is an undeclared repetition'),[68] if there is a task *specific* to politics, it must be to find clear and universal principles of justice that *break* with the infinite complexities and complicities of history, the interminable 'negotiations' of culture and psychology. And thereby to allow something *else* to take place.

V Open questions

L'Ethique is an enormously engaging book. Badiou provides an inspiring, rigorously argued alternative to the tired moralizing truisms of neo-Kantian universalism on the one hand, and a more or less tolerant liberal-communitarianism on the other. Badiou's uncompromising emphasis on subjective *commitment* and his unabashedly militant priorities infuse his work with a trenchant, exhilarating audacity seldom risked in our post-Leninist times. His ethic of truths may prove to be the most provocative contemporary challenge to the reigning orthodoxies of a moralizing 'cultural studies' informed by the valorization of difference and marginality. His systematic reformulation of the concepts of subject, being, event, situation, materialism, engagement – and even of truth itself – will deserve careful, detailed evaluation.

So concise an intervention is bound, of course, to leave a number of fairly substantial questions unanswered. In what

remains of this Introduction I would like to mention two
such questions in particular (both of which are certain to
receive more developed treatment in Badiou's current and
future work).

(a) Does Badiou's theory fully account for the specificity of situations?

Like any 'interventionist' philosophy (that of Marx, Freud,
Lenin, Sartre . . .), Badiou's militant conception of truths
presumes a well-defined theory of *situation*. It is an essential
point of principle that 'all humanity has its root in the
identification in thought [*en pensée*] of singular situations'.[69]
Whatever the circumstances, a truth is something that *takes
place* at a particular time and under particular circumstances: 'to enter into the composition of a subject of truth
can only be something that *happens to you*'.[70] A truth is not
only specified by its occasion (and an event is itself located
within the stuation by its *site*, i.e. its proximity to the 'void'
of the situation), it *is*, it *composes*, an ongoing production
that is entirely internal to the situation. The situated quality
of Badiou's theory certainly sets it apart from the altogether
less precise musings on 'community', 'politics' and 'ethics'
proposed by some of his better-known neo-Heideggerian
contemporaries and rivals (Nancy, Lacoue-Labarthe, Agam-
ben, Derrida again . . .).

Badiou's equation of the general notion of 'situation'
with the mathematical notion of *set* [*ensemble*], however,
undercuts in some ways his claim to grasp the specificity of
any particular situation. The set-theoretic approach ensures
that a situation is defined exclusively by what *belongs* to
it (its elements, or members), without reference to the

constituent *relations* that might exist among these elements (in set theory, the very notion of 'constituent' relations is a contradiction in terms). The situation as such is made up simply of its elements, considered in their solitary ontological isolation (as x, y, z ...). The state of the situation – which in pertinent situations will include, but far exceed, political state – is what then groups and links these elements in the combinations that contribute to the ordering of the situation (say, x grouped with y as members of the same economic class, political party, tax bracket, postal district, etc.). This distinction of situation and state is fundamental to Badiou's whole conception of truth. By aligning the whole dimension of relationality on the side of the state, he lends the situation an effectively limitless indetermination. Such is the basis of the situation's 'infinite possibility'.[71]

Arguably, however, Badiou's consequent characterization of all human situations, individual and collective, as *immeasurably* infinite multiplicities (and thus as bundles of pure and immeasurable 'differences', such that 'there are as many differences, say, between a Chinese peasant and a young Norwegian professional as between myself and anybody at all, including myself')[72] dramatically *simplifies* these situations, leaving no space for the acknowledgement of effectively universal structuring principles (biological, cognitive, linguistic ...) on the one hand, or of certain 'specifying' attributes (based on culture, religion, class, gender ...) on the other. Instead, we are left with 'generic human stuff' that is ontologically indistinguishable from pure mathematical multiplicity and effectively endowed, in its praxis, with a kind of indeterminate 'fundamental freedom'. (We might say that if the 'generic' indetermination of the situation corresponds to some degree with Sartre's

pure freedom or praxis, then its state effectively occupies
the vast conceptual space Sartre embraced under the concept of the 'practico-inert'). The potential risk, as I have
suggested elsewhere, is the effective 'despecification' (or
'singularization') of situations in general, to say nothing of
the truth-processes that 'puncture' them.[73] Some readers
might prefer to settle for a slightly more 'impure' range of
possibility were it informed by a more determinate, more
specific understanding of the situation as such.

(b) Does Badiou have a sustainable theory of ethical *deliberation?*

My second question concerns the relative contingency of
the ethical *procedure* as such. Engagement in truth is essentially a matter of axiomatic intervention, an effectively
immediate decision for or against the event (more precisely,
'for', or 'against' the connection of this or that element of
the situation to the event). But Badiou naturally wants to
avoid a simply dictatorial model of subjective engagement,
however logical its dictation. What sort of critical or reflexive distance is presumed, then, by any subjective intervention? The problem becomes especially acute once we are
dealing, as in every political situation, with more than one
individual. Badiou's response is to accept *some* sort of deliberative procedure, while insisting that such a procedure
arises in each case as fully internal to its situation.

> As a general rule, every generic procedure is in reality a process
> that can perfectly well be deliberative, as long as we understand
> that *it invents its rule of deliberation at the same time as it invents
> itself.* And it is no more constrained by a pre-established norm

xxxiv   TRANSLATOR'S INTRODUCTION

that follows from the rule of deliberation. You have only to look at how the rule of deliberation in different organizations, in different political sequences, and in different political modes, is entirely variable. . . . Every time a plurality of individuals, a plurality of human subjects, is engaged in a process of truth, the construction of this process induces the construction of a deliberative and collective figure of this production, which is itself variable.[74]

But the whole question is precisely whether such delibera-tion is *variable*, in the sense of so many variations on some kind of minimally invariant process, or forever *different*, in the sense of so many inventions *ex nihilo*, each one literally peculiar to a given procedure. This is where Badiou might have to engage with the broadly Habermasian elaboration of a 'quasi-transcendental' schema of communicative rational-ity – the minimum upon which we must all agree, *so as to be able to disagree* (in any particular case). For where exactly are we to draw the line between the sort of strictly *subjective* deliberation that is internal to the elaboration of a truth, and a merely ideological opposition? Both of Badiou's most insistent examples, Leninist and Jacobin, testify to the uncer-tainty of such a line as much as they illustrate an inventive approach to the resolution of disagreement and debate.

More generally, if some degree of 'un-binding', some kind of break with the past, some degree of distance from the inertia of the status quo, are clearly essential to any 'emancipatory' innovation, the question remains: can these distancings be described and assessed in more 'relational' (and thus more 'specific') terms than those of *rupture* and *soustraction*? If every truth proceeds as a generalized *dé-liaison* or un-linking, if every subject is a 'subject given over to the anguish of non-relation [*non-lien*]',[75] might the rela-

tions at work in the very process of *dé-liaison* itself be
accounted for in a philosophy orientated to the *constitutively
situated* dimension of all being? This is perhaps the most
important of the several questions that Badiou's current
work in progress promises to address.[76]

In the meantime, Badiou's incisive contribution to perhaps
the most oversaturated field of contemporary philosophical
and cultural inquiry amounts to far more than a 'timely
clarification of the issues' or an 'invigorating reconfigura-
tion of the problem'. Badiou's book does nothing less than
evacuate the foundation upon which every deconstructive,
'multicultural' or 'postcolonial' ethics is built: the (ethical)
category of alterity. The whole tangled body of doctrine
variously associated with the *Other* – and developed by
Lévinas, Derrida, Irigaray, and Spivak, among so many
'others' – is here simply swept away. Gone is the complex
'negotiation' of a multiplicity of shifting 'subject positions'.
Gone is any recourse to 'strategic essentialism'. Gone is the
whole abject register of 'bearing witness', of a guilt-driven
empathy or compassion ultimately indistinguishable from a
distanced condescension. Gone are the anguished musings
of an 'irreplaceable' subject confronted with the impossibly
demanding needs of the Altogether-Other (or the impossibly inconsistent demands of many others). Gone is the
tension between this irreplaceable subjectivity and the
'temptation' to justify action according to indifferent criteria of universal validity (which thereby 'threaten' the subject
with replacement). Gone is the tortured reflexive logic of a
'decision made by the other in me'. Gone is the anti-
philosophical conviction that only the Altogether-Other can

'know' and validate this decision. Gone is the ultimately
theological basis for this otherness. Gone is the pathos of
finitude, the tragic obligations of the 'hostage' and the
'sacrifice'. Gone is the paralysing recognition of a *generalized*
'impossibility'. Gone, in short, is the theoretical association
of ethics with a 'goodness too good for this world', along
with its practical (legal) justification of this same world.

With Badiou, the Other (or others) is not an ethical
category, for the simple reason that infinite multiplicity is
the very medium of being itself. Radical difference is a
matter of ethical indifference. The ethical decision *holds
true* only if it is indifferent to differences. And the subject of
the ethical or truthful decision *becomes* a subject – becomes
irreplaceable, or singular in Derrida's sense – only when he
or she engages in that decision. It is the very engagement
in truth that retrospectively 'induces' a singular, irreplaceable subject, 'in the body' of what was previously an indifferent individual. Every rigorously singular procedure
articulates a thoroughly *generic* truth. *There can be no irreplaceable subject without engagement in a process in which, in principle,
any subject might take part.*

This book extends an invitation, indifferently addressed,
to take up such a part.

Notes

1. Where a reference contains two page numbers separated by
   a forward slash, the first number refers to the original edition
   and the second to the translation listed in the bibliography,
   section B; 'tm' stands for 'translation modified'.
2. For a relatively thorough study, see Peter Hallward, *Subject to
   Truth: An Introduction to the Philosophy of Alain Badiou* (forth-

coming from Minnesota University Press, 2001). Shorter surveys include Slavoj Žižek, 'Psychoanalysis in Post-Marxism: The Case of Alain Badiou' (1998), reprinted and extended in Žižek, *The Ticklish Subject* (1999); Jean-Jacques Lecercle, 'Cantor, Lacan, Mao, Beckett, *même combat*: The Philosophy of Alain Badiou' (1999); Peter Hallward, 'Generic Sovereignty: The Philosophy of Alain Badiou' (1998). See the Bibliography for a list of translations of Badiou's works.

3. See Alain Badiou, *L'Etre et l'événement*, 374, 430.

4. On the void, see Note 7 below.

5. *L'Ethique*, 77/87 (the second number refers to the present edition).

6. The (fairly complex) justification for this assertion is provided in *L'Etre et l'événement*. The basic argument runs as follows. First of all, Badiou *assumes* that there is no God, that is, no all-embracing One. And if the One is not, then what there *is* must simply be pure multiplicity, that is, *multiples without units*, or multiples of multiples. The upshot is the effective equation of ontology, the discourse of pure *being-qua-being*, with the discourse of pure mathematics. (More precisely, Badiou equates ontology with modern *set* theory, i.e. that part of mathematics which accounts for the derivation and nature, or 'being', of mathematical entities and operations.) In other words, mathematics is the discourse that 'articulates' what remains of being when all other qualities and characteristics – materiality, shape, texture, colour, intensity . . . – have been abstracted, so as to isolate *pure* being-*qua*-being (or *pure* multiplicity, uncontaminated by any sense or substance). Badiou's mathematized articulation of being has little technical impact on the present book. What matters is the conclusion Badiou draws, rather quickly, from his fundamental ontological 'axioms': all situations can be defined as 'infinite multiples', that is, as sets with an infinite number of elements. And what 'relate' these elements, *qua* elements, are only relations of pure difference (or indifference): x as different from y.

7. The concept of the void of the situation is another difficult and important point developed in detail in *L'Etre et l'événement*. The guiding idea is that what determines 'normality' in a situation is its particular manner of foreclosing, in something like the Lacanian sense, its minimally defined, minimally 'differed' part. The 'void' of the situation is what eludes representation by the state of the situation (for example: the proletariat in capitalist situations, or 'illegal' immigrants in 'Western' situations). What then *situates* an event – what determines what Badiou calls its 'evental site [*site événementiel*]' – is its location at 'the edge of the void' of the situation in which it takes place. More technically, the site is an element of the situation which itself, counted from the perspective of the situation, has no distinguishable elements or members of its own, and thus seems 'void' from that perspective (the proletarian 'mob', the mass of 'faceless' immigrants . . .).

8. Jacques Lacan, *Séminaire VII*, 362–8/314–19.

9. Ibid., 270/230.

10. See Slavoj Žižek, *Tarrying with the Negative*, 97; *Metastases of Enjoyment*, 201. The implications of a Lacanian approach to ethics are brilliantly developed by Alenka Zupančič in her book *Ethics of the Real* (2000), which owes much to Badiou's conception of things (Badiou uses the phrase *éthique du réel* on page 52 below).

11. Lacan, *Séminaire VII*, 20–21/11; emphasis added.

12. Jacques Lacan, *Séminaire XI*, 64/53.

13. Jacques Lacan, *Ecrits*, 302/88; emphasis added. Just as Badiou sees the constitution of a subject in terms of its articulation of a truth, so the goal of psychoanalysis is 'to teach the subject to name, to articulate, to bring this desire into existence. . . . It isn't a question of recognizing something which would be entirely given [in advance . . .:] in naming it, the subject creates, brings forth, a new presence in the world' (Lacan, *Séminaire II*, 267/228–9).

14. Samuel Beckett, *L'Innommable*, 213. With Beckett, 'nothing begins that is not in the prescription of the again or of the re-beginning' (Alain Badiou, *Petit manuel d'inesthéthique*, 140).

15. 'Anti-philosophical', Lacan's own self-description, is a label used by Badiou to indicate, negatively, a fundamental resistance to conceptual explanation, and positively, a faith in some kind of ineffable, transcendent Meaning, grasped in the active subtraction of *philosophical* pretensions to truth. As the great anti-philosopher Pascal put it, to mock or 'dismiss philosophy is to be a true philosopher' (Blaise Pascal, *Pensées*, para. 24 [4], in *Oeuvres*, 1095). For since (divine) truth is a function of the 'heart', a matter of faith and direct intuition, so for Pascal 'the final achievement of reason is the recognition that there are an infinity of things that surpass its power' (*Pensées*, 267). For the anti-philosopher, true value holds itself aloof in a pure, 'supraphilosophical' event or act, in 'a thinking more rigorous than the conceptual' (Martin Heidegger, 'Letter on Humanism', in *Basic Writings*, 258). In short, anti-philosophy relies on a 'silent supra-cognitive or mystical intuition' (Alain Badiou, *Deleuze*, 31). Badiou maintains that philosophy should generally engage as closely as possible with the great anti-philosophers, in order to *refute* them.

   Saint Paul's 'discourse of Life' (as opposed to the pretensions of Greek philosophy); Pascal's *charité* (against rational and institutional intellect); Rousseau's sincerity (against the science of Voltaire and the Encyclopédistes); Kierkegaard's redemptive choice (against Hegel's synthesis); Nietzsche's 'active' force (against the 'theoretical' *ressentiment* of the philosopher-priest); the early Wittgenstein's inarticulable, otherworldly Meaning (against speculative idealism); Heidegger's letting-be (against the technocratic manipulation of beings) – these are all so many efforts to set an ineffable *Value* against mere theory, a genuine *Act* against the feeble abstractions of philosophy (see Alain Badiou, *Saint Paul*, 62).

Showing here prevails over *saying*: anti-philosophy reveals, where philosophy explains. Every 'anti-philosophical act consists of letting become apparent "what there is", to the degree that "what there is" is precisely that which no proposition is able to say' (Alain Badiou, 'Silence, solipsisme, sainteté', 17).

Lacan's own anti-philosophical orientation is guaranteed by the fact that his subject is derivative of some deeper, ultimately inaccessible (unconscious) force – first desire, then drive. Neither can be reduced to concepts. In either case, famously, 'whatever it is, I must go there, because, somewhere, [the] unconscious *reveals* itself' (Lacan, *Séminaire XI*, 41/33; emphasis added). And because Lacan's subject is *primarily* that which flickers through cracks in the structures of social consensus and psychological normalization, analysis always risks its reduction to a quasi-contemplative *recognition* of the perverse 'particularity of the subject' (as a gap in the Other, as the phantom puppet of *objet a*, as *driven* by its own *jouissance*...). Unlike Badiou, Lacan holds that 'the dimension of truth is mysterious, inexplicable' (*Séminaire III*, 214/214), that desire is constitutively elusive (*Séminaire XX*, 71), that the Real is essentially a matter of ambivalence and loss, that analysis is steeped in the *tragic* and *horrific* dimensions of mortal experience ...

16. Alain Badiou, 'Politics and Philosophy', Appendix to this volume, p. 121. 'Thought is not a relation to an object, it is the *internal* relation of its Real [*rapport interne de son réel*]' (Alain Badiou, *Abrégé de métapolitique*, 37; see also *Théorie du sujet*, 146–7).

17. Badiou, *Saint Paul*, 60. The proletariat, for instance, is that Real un-represented element upon which the capitalist situation is built, just as the *sans-papiers* ('illegal' immigrants) currently occupy the absent centre of current debates on the nature of France as a political community. In keeping with this conception of the Real, what Badiou will call 'emancipatory politics always consists in making seem possible precisely

that which, from within the situation, is declared to be impossible' ('Politics and Philosophy', below, p. 121) – the empowerment of the proletariat, the legalization of immigrants. . . .

18. Žižek, *Ticklish Subject*, 160, 154. Subsequent references to page numbers in this work appear in brackets in the text.

19. Lacan, *Séminaire II*, 270–71/232–3, in Žižek, *Ticklish Subject*, 155, 160. Like Badiou after him, Lacan insists that 'behind what is named, there is the unnameable'. But for the analyst, as opposed to the philosopher, the 'quintessential unnameable [is] death' (*Séminaire II*, 247/211). From a Lacanian perspective, 'the function of desire must remain in a fundamental relationship to death' (*Séminaire VII*, 351/303) – that is, it must remain within a properly *tragic* dimension (361/313). A (Lacanian) emphasis on the structural 'regularity' of the subject, in other words, orientates it towards the mere cessation of that structure – whereas Badiou's 'exceptionality' makes a break with mortality *tout court*.

20. Žižek, *The Ticklish Subject*, 155.

21. Zupančič's *Ethics of the Real* again provides valuable material for the development of this comparison.

22. Immanuel Kant, *Groundwork of the Metaphysics of Morals*, 443. Subsequent references to page numbers in this work appear in brackets in the text.

23. Žižek, *Plague*, 221; see also Lacan, *Séminaire VII*, 364/315.

24. Kant, *Groundwork*, 391.

25. Immanuel Kant, *Critique of Practical Reason*, 91–2.

26. Immanuel Kant, *Critique of Pure Reason*, Bxxx, A641–642/B669–670, A828/B856.

27. Kant, *Groundwork*, 390.

28. Emmanuel Lévinas, *Basic Philosophical Writings*, 53. See Badiou, *L'Ethique*, ch. 2 below.

29. Lévinas, *Totalité et infini*, 23/24. 'In welcoming the Other I welcome the Most High to which my freedom is subordinated' (335/300tm).

30. Lévinas, 'Transcendence and Height', in *Basic Philosophical Writings*, 19; see also Emmanuel Lévinas, *Autrement qu'être*, 173–88/110–18.

31. Lévinas, 'Substitution', in *Basic Philosophical Writings*, 91. Very simply, 'subjectivity is ... subjection to the other [*autrui*]' (140) that is, to a properly absolute authority. 'I expose myself to the summons of this responsibility as though placed under a blazing sun that eradicates every residue of mystery, every ulterior motive, every loosening of the thread that would allow evasion' (104).

32. Lévinas, 'Transcendence and Height', in *Basic Philosophical Writings*, 16.

33. 'If decision-making is relegated to a knowledge that it is content to follow or to develop, then it is no more a responsible decision, it is the technical deployment of a cognitive apparatus, the simple mechanistic deployment of a theorem...: there is no responsibility without a dissident and inventive rupture with respect to tradition, authority, orthodoxy' (Jacques Derrida, *Donner la mort*, 31/24, 33–4/27; see also Jacques Derrida, *Adieu à Emmanuel Lévinas*, 199–200).

34. See, for instance, Jacques Derrida, *Donner le temps*, 26–7; 45–8, 52–3.

35. Derrida, *Donner la mort*, 68/68, 76–7/78; ibid., ch. 4.

36. Derrida, *Donner la mort*, 83–4/87. This confusion 'opens the space and introduces the hope of salvation [*du salut*]' (84/87: subsequent references to page numbers in this work appear in brackets in the text).

37. Thus 'God is in me, he is the absolute "me" or "self", he is that structure of invisible interiority that is called, in Kierkegaard's sense, subjectivity. And he is made manifest, he manifests his nonmanifestation when, in the structures of the living or the entity, there appears in the course of phylo- and ontogenetic history, the possibility of secrecy', that is, 'a structure of conscience' organized around the mysterious

presence of an interior 'witness that others cannot see' and that I cannot know, a 'secret witnessing within me' (Derrida, *Donner la mort*, 101–2/108–9). From here it is a (very) short step to the restoration of a perfectly classical notion of conscience or *inner surveillance*, of the Other 'looking in' on me (Derrida, speaking at the conference 'Derrida's Arguments', Queen Mary & Westfield College, University of London, 10 March 2000).

38. 'To pose the Inaccessible as Inaccessible, and so to open the way to an infinite hermeneutics, is the religious position *par excellence*' (Badiou, letter to Peter Hallward, 19 June 1996; see also Alain Badiou, *Conditions*, 69; *Monde contemporain et désir de philosophie*, 16). It is important not to confuse Derrida's *secret* with Badiou's *unnameable*. There is nothing secret or inaccessible about the unnameable element as such; there is nothing to stop us *knowing* it or exchanging opinions regarding it (Badiou, *L'Ethique*, 76–7/86). The unnameable is unnameable only from within the truth-procedure. The unnameable simply indicates the limit where, for a subject to continue as part of a truth-process, he or she must exercise *restraint*. Badiou's precisely situated unnameable is incommensurable with Derrida's 'name of God as completely other, the nameless name of God, the unpronounceable name of God as other to which I am bound by an absolute, unconditional obligation' (Derrida, *Donner la mort*, 67/67).

39. Derrida, *Donner la mort*, 14–15/5.

40. Ibid., 62/61.

41. Derrida, *Adieu à Emmanuel Lévinas*, 87; 'Intellectual Courage: An Interview' [1998], http://culturemachine.tees.ac.uk/frm_f1.htm, p. 5.

42. Derrida, *Donner la mort*, 58/56 (referring to Kierkegaard and Patočka). And for the same reason, only the other can *know* if such a decision ocurs; only *God knows*, literally, if a decision occurs.

43. Ibid., 62/61.

44. Badiou, *L'Ethique*, 39/43.

45. Derrida, *Donner la mort*, 67/66.

46. Lacan, *Séminaire XX*, 100. No one has taken more seriously than Badiou Lacan's declaration that 'mathematical formalization is our goal, our ideal' (ibid., 108; see also Lacan, *Ecrits*, 816/314; Badiou, *Conditions*, 292, 322). With far more systematic rigour than his mentor, Badiou will continue to argue that 'the grasp of thought upon the Real can be established only by the regulated power of the letter – a regulation which only mathematics can perfect' (Alain Badiou, 'Lacan et les présocratiques' [1990], 4).

47. Badiou maintains, against all invocations of anti-philosophical 'sincerity', that 'philosophy has never been possible without accepting the possibility of an anonymous statement', that is, without the production of statements that compel examination 'in their own right' (Alain Badiou, *Casser en deux l'histoire du monde?*, 17).

48. Badiou, *Abrégé de métapolitique*, 12; see also *Monde contemporain et désir de philosophie*, 5–6.

49. 'The future can only be anticipated in the form of absolute danger. It is what breaks absolutely with constituted normality and can only be proclaimed, presented, as a kind of monstrosity' (Jacques Derrida, *De la grammatologie*, 14/5; see also *L'Ecriture et la différence*, 428/293; *Points de suspension*, 401). Whereas the whole effort of Badiou's theory of the event is geared around the question of its *site*, Derrida's event is unsituated, 'without horizon' (Jacques Derrida, *Sur Parole*, 49–50).

50. Gilles Deleuze, *Logique du sens*, 355–7/305–6.

51. Luce Irigaray, 'Questions for Emmanuel Levinas', in *Irigaray Reader*, 180.

52. Luce Irigaray, *Temps*, 32/14.

53. Ibid., 16/xvi.

54. Luce Irigaray, *Sexes et parentés*, 93/79.

55. Luce Irigaray, *Je, Tu, Nous*, 25/22.

56. Ibid., 108/86; see also 'The Necessity for Sexuate Rights', in *Irigaray Reader*, 198–203.

57. 'In a woman('s) language, the concept as such would have no place' (Luce Irigaray, *Ce sexe*, 122/122–3; see also Luce Irigaray, *Speculum*, 177–8/142–3). The 'truly' feminine eludes conceptual precision by definition – 'there is simply no way I can give you an account of "speaking (as) woman"'; it is spoken, but not in conventionally theoretical or 'philosophical' language (*Ce sexe*, 141/144). Throughout Irigaray's work, women are associated with typically anti-philosophical themes (divine, angelic, ethereal, liminal, aesthetic, and so on). An especially important part of the assertion of a 'specific culture for women' is the call for 'divine representation', female gods affirming women as women, as 'beautiful and slim', and so on. 'The loss of divine representation . . . has left us without a means of designating ourselves, of expressing ourselves, between ourselves' (Luce Irigaray, *Je, Tu, Nous*, 135/111). As this outcome implies, the anti-philosophical critique of philosophical 'mastery', so central to Irigaray's early work, does not preclude an abundance of alternative identity prescriptions: 'women *must* cultivate a double identity: virgins and mothers' (*Je, Tu, Nous*, 142/117tm); 'women *must* love one another both as mothers and as daughters', and so on (Luce Irigaray, *Ethique*, 103/105; emphasis added).

58. Irigaray, *Je, Tu, Nous*, 110/88.

59. Irigaray, *Temps*, 121/109.

60. Ibid., 28/10.

61. In due course, Irigaray carries her logic to its proper conclusion: to seek equality as a general goal is in itself 'a grave ethical fault', one that contributes to the 'erasure of natural and spiritual reality' (Luce Irigaray, *J'aime à toi*, 53–4/27; see also 'How to Define Sexuate Rights', in *Irigaray Reader*, 206).

62. Gayatri Chakravorty Spivak, *The Critique of Postcolonial Reason*, 175.

63. Ibid., 198; Gayatri Chakravorty Spivak, 'Love, Cruelty and Cultural Talks in the Hot Peace', 11; see also Spivak, *Critique*, 383–4; 399; 426. The word 'subaltern' is to be 'reserved for the sheer heterogeneity of decolonized space' (*Critique*, 310), which seems to evoke something like absolute alterity (*vis-à-vis*, presumably, Spivak's supposed readership).

64. Gayatri Chakravorty Spivak, 'In the New World Order', 92; 'What Is It For?', 79; see also *Outside in the Teaching Machine*, 175–7.

65. Gayatri Chakravorty Spivak, 'Translator's Preface to Mashaweta Devi, *Imaginary Maps*', *Spivak Reader*, 269.

66. Gayatri Chakravorty Spivak, 'Diasporas Old and New', 258.

67. Gayatri Chakravorty Spivak, 'Translator's Afterword to Mashaweta Devi, *Imaginary Maps*', *Spivak Reader*, 274; see also *Critique*, 246.

68. Spivak, *Critique*, 333.

69. Badiou, *L'Ethique*, 18/16.

70. Ibid., 47/51.

71. Badiou, 'What Is a Political Truth?', talk given at the Maison française, Oxford (2 March 2000).

72. Badiou, *L'Ethique*, 26/26.

73. See Hallward, *Subject to Truth*, ch. 13.

74. 'Politics and Philosophy', below, p. 117; emphasis added. 'A singular truth is always the result of a complex process, in which discussion is decisive. Science itself began – with mathematics – by renouncing all principles of authority. Scientific statements are precisely those exposed, naked, to public criticism, independently of the subject of their enunciation.' Against Arendt, Badiou insists that discussion can be privileged *over* truth only if a 'right to discussion' is a right reserved for 'falsehood and lies' (*Abrégé de métapolitique*, 24). And as far as practical politics is concerned, 'discussion is political only to the degree that it crystallizes in a decision' (24).

75. Badiou, *Conditions*, 120. Such is our 'modern ascesis: to

expose thought to *dé-liaison* pure and simple' (Badiou, *Deleuze*, 123).

76. It is this question that Badiou is currently exploring in his analysis, informed by topos theory and Heyting algebra, of 'appearing' or 'being-there [*être-là*]'. See Alain Badiou, *Court traité d'ontologie transitoire* (1998), chs 9, 13, 14; 'L'Etre-là: mathématique du transcendental' (unpublished, 2000); Hallward, *Subject to Truth*, ch. 14.

Notes on the Translation

As a matter of emphatic principle, Badiou's philosophy is designed to be as indifferent as possible to the language in which it is conveyed. Most of the problems encountered in translating *L'Ethique* concern only its remarkable concision and frequent abstraction; there are just a few terms and stylistic choices that deserve special mention.

With Badiou's consent, and for the sake of clarity, I have distinguished the always singular 'ethic of truths [*l'éthique des vérités*]' from 'ethics [*l'éthique*]' in its conventional – and here pejorative – sense. Every other important element of Badiou's terminology – *truth, truth-process* [*processus de vérité*], *event, subject, being, situation, fidelity, void* [*vide*] – has been translated as literally as possible, even when (as occasionally with 'void' and 'fidelity') these terms jar with normal English usage. I have had recourse to the slightly clumsy neologism 'evental' to translate his use of the word '*événementiel*', which has little to do with either the conventional meaning of 'factual' or the connotation made famous by Fernand Braudel and the *Annales* approach to historiography; to my mind, the more natural choice of 'eventful' by Madarasz and Burchill in their translations of Badiou's *Manifesto* and *Deleuze* invites misleading associations (plenitude, bustle, familiarity), while simply to adopt the French word as is (on the model of Lacan's *jouissance*) would be to concede too much to those principles of linguistic 'constructivism' and particularism that Badiou's universalism so vigorously rejects. *Un ensemble* is usually translated by mathematicians as a *set*, and I have generally followed suit; the reader should remember, however, that the English word loses the notion of 'being-together' or 'collectivity' implied by the French. The awkward-sounding 'multiple-being' translates Badiou's *être-multiple*, which is synonymous with what he analyses, in *L'Etre et l'événement*, as pure being-*qua*-being [*l'être-en-tant-qu'être*]: this refers to the being of any indifferent thing considered in isolation from its every substantial or describable quality – that is, being reduced to *purely* ontological characteristics, which Badiou equates with the characteristics of multiplicity as such.

Readers of French will be familiar with the double meaning of the word *droit* (both law and right, as in human right); though the context has usually encouraged its translation as *right* or *rights*, it is in large part the legal orientation of the term that attracts Badiou's scorn. The words *penser* and *pensée* are more difficult to render in suitably solemn English: to conceive, to conceptualize, and so on, are all off the mark, and for all their apparent naivety, 'to think' and 'thought' are usually the only viable options. It should be remembered that for Badiou, *thinking* is an activity reserved to the field of truths, and it should never be confused with the effectively 'thoughtless' expression of recognized opinions or the (state-driven) manipulation of representations.

Finally, for the sake of syntactical simplicity and with apologies to readers irritated by such conventions, I have preserved the standard French use of masculine pronouns and the generic term 'man' [*l'homme* or *l'Homme*].

Translator's notes have been kept to a minimum, and are distinguished by enclosure in square brackets; all other notes are Badiou's own.

Thanks to all those who helped with the translation: Sepideh Anvar, Gillian Beaumont, Patrick ffrench, Cécile Laborde, Sinéad Rushe, John Taylor, and of course, Alain Badiou himself.

Preface to the English Edition

The story of this book is peculiar. It actually began as a commission, as part of a series aimed at secondary-school and university students. I agreed to write it out of friendship for the man behind the project, Benoît Chantre, one of today's few editors worthy of the name. I wrote it in the countryside, in the summer of 1993, in the space of two weeks, stimulated by a constant stream of phone-calls from this same Benoît Chantre. My approach at the time thus conformed to that of an exercise whose rules are imposed from the outside: a fixed word-limit, the need to remain accessible to a non-specialized readership, the obligation to refer to current affairs, and so on.

All the same, the real difficulty lay elsewhere. It sprang from a contradictory state of mind. On the one hand, I was driven by a genuine fury. The world was deeply plunged in 'ethical' delirium. Everyone was busily confusing politics with the hypocrisy of a mindless catechism. The intellectual counter-revolution, in the form of moral terrorism, was imposing the infamies of Western capitalism as the new universal model. The presumed 'rights of man' were serving at every point to annihilate any attempt to invent forms of free thought. As a result, my book became something of a pamphlet. On a number of occasions my editor and friend had to ask me to tone down my invective. On the other hand, however, some of the questions raised in the book called for a subtle and inventive discipline of thought. I had still not yet drawn all the practical consequences – and ethical consequences, for that matter – of the ontology of truths I had put forward five years earlier, in *L'Etre et l'événement* (1988), so that even for me, a good number of the points developed in the present book were new and uncertain.

I was thus caught between the simplifying temptations of the pamphleteer and the necessary rigour of conceptual innovation. The solution – if it was a solution – was to dilute the ideological fury bit by bit over the course of the philosophical construction. As it stands, the book begins as a political attack against the ideology of human rights, and as a defence of the antihumanism of the 1960s. It closes by sketching an ethic of truths, in which I distinguish from the human animal (whose 'rights' are not easily identified) the subject as such, the subject understood as the local fragment of a truth-procedure, and as the immortal creation of an event.

What is most surprising is that this slightly strange combination of fighting against the ideological current (moralism, a generalized victimization, was at the time a matter of *consensus*) and conceptual schematizaton enjoyed considerable success, not least in secondary schools. To date, along with *Manifesto for Philosophy*, *Ethics* is my bestselling book. As sometimes happens, a good many people were grateful that I had taken the risk of saying frankly something that is uncomfortable to say. And these same people – and perhaps others too – also know that I take this risk only from the standpoint of a genuine philosophical enterprise, for truly pressing reasons, and not simply to draw attention to myself. The truth is, incidentally, that I am much too shy to enjoy drawing attention to myself.

Today I can look at this book, which came out almost seven years ago, from two different angles: that of the ideological polemic, and that of the theoretical construction.

As regards the first angle, I have no regrets. We have since had to endure the intervention of Western bombers against Serbia, the intolerable blockade of Iraq, the continuation of threats against Cuba. All of this is still legitimated by a quite unbelievable outpouring of moralizing sermons. The International Tribunal is clearly prepared to arrest and try, in the name of 'human rights', anyone, anywhere, who attempts to contest the New World Order of which NATO (i.e. the United States) is the armed guard. Today, our 'democratic' totalitarianism is all the more firmly entrenched. It is now more necessary than ever that those with free minds rise up against this servile way of thinking, against this miserable moralism in the name of which we are obliged to accept the prevailing way of the world and its absolute injustice. The most that can be said is that perhaps the *consensus* is slowly weakening. The intervention against Serbia did at least provoke a debate, a debate which never really took place regarding Bosnia or Iraq. American imperialism and European servility are denounced more often now than they were a few years ago. To be sure, the enemy, comforted by the collapse of authoritarian socialism, dominates everywhere. But it is also true that we are entering into a long period of recomposition, both for emancipatory political thought and for those effective practical forces that correspond to it. We are in a position to declare, as the complementary watchwords of this recomposition, the two essential prescriptions of the day: the dissolution of NATO, and the disbanding of the International Court of Human Rights.

As for the theoretical construction, it must be said that the ideas of this little book, although they are orientated in the right direction, constitute no more than a preliminary sketch. I am currently in the process of developing them, and sometimes modifying them, with respect to at least four points.

1. The concept of situation is especially important, since I maintain that there can be no ethics in general, but only an ethic of singular truths, and thus an ethic relative to a particular situation. I now accept that a situation cannot be understood simply as a multiple [i.e. as a set]. We must also take into account the network of relations it sustains, which involves making sense of the way a multiple appears in the situation. This means that a situation must be conceived as both, in its *being*, a pure multiple (in keeping with the argument of *L'Etre et l'événement*) and, in its *appearing*, as the effect of a transcendental legislation. All this will be developed in my forthcoming book, entitled *Logiques du monde* [*Logics of the World*], which I conceive as the sequel to *L'Etre et l'événement*.

2. Today I can no longer maintain that the only trace left by an event in the situation it affects is the name given to that event. This idea presumed, in effect, that there were two events rather than one (the event-event and the event-naming), and likewise two subjects rather than one (the subject who names the event, and the subject who is faithful to this naming). So I now posit that an event is implicative,

in the sense that it enables the detachment of a statement which will subsist as such once the event itself has disappeared. This statement was previously undecided, or of an uncertain value. When it takes place, the event decides its value (it determines its truthfulness and, in so doing, modifies the entire logic of the situation (its entire transcendental regime). Here again, in other words, the ontological theory of the event needs to be completed by a logical theory. These points were developed in detail in my seminars of 1996–97 and 1997–98, and will be reworked in *Logiques du monde.*

3. The subject cannot be conceived exclusively as the subject faithful to the event. This point in particular has significant ethical implications. For I was previously unable to explain the appearance of reactionary innovations. My whole theory of the new confined it to the truth-procedures. But when all is said and done, it is obvious that reaction, and even the powers of death, can be stamped with the creative force of an event. I had already emphasized the fact that Nazism was inexplicable without reference to communism, and more precisely to the Revolution of October 1917. I was then obliged to admit that the event opens a subjective space in which not only the progressive and truthful subjective figure of fidelity but also other figures every bit as innovative, albeit negative – such as the reactive figure, or the figure I call the 'obscure subject' – take their place.

4. The trajectory of a truth, finally, should not be referred back solely to the multiple consistency of the situation, nor to its 'encyclopaedia of knowledges'. We need to understand how it deals with logical transformations. This brings us back to the question of how truths *appear*, whereas up to

this point I had considered only their being (i.e. the fact that truths are generic multiplicities).

So you can see that the theoretical basis of the present book has evolved somewhat. But to my mind it remains solid enough on the essential points, and still offers an introduction that is both lively and coherent to a far-reaching enterprise which, I hope, will redefine what is at stake in contemporary philosophy.

I do not want to end without thanking both Verso, for their intellectual and political commitment, and Peter Hallward, who is a genuine friend – and all the more so since he often disagrees with my theories.

Alain Badiou, April 2000

Introduction

Certain scholarly words, after long confinement in diction-
aries and in academic prose, have the good fortune, or the
misfortune – a little like an old maid who, long since resigned
to her fate, suddenly becomes, without understanding why,
the toast of the town – of sudden exposure to the bright light
of day, of being plebi- and publi-cited, press-released, tele-
vised, even mentioned in government speeches. The word
ethics, which smacks so strongly of philosophy courses and its
Greek root, which evokes Aristotle (*The Nicomachean Ethics*,
one of the great bestsellers!), has today taken centre stage.

Ethics concerns, in Greek, the search for a good 'way of
being', for a wise course of action. On this account, ethics
is a part of philosophy, that part which organizes practical
existence around representation of the Good.

The Stoics were no doubt the most dedicated of those
who made of ethics not only a part of philosophical wisdom
but its *very core*. The wise man is he who, able to distinguish
those things which are his responsibility from those which
are not, restricts his will to the former while impassively
enduring the latter. We attribute to the Stoics, moreover,
the custom of comparing philosophy to an egg whose shell
is Logic, whose white is Physics, and whose yolk is Ethics.

With the moderns – for whom, since Descartes, the
question of the subject has been central – ethics is more or
less synonymous with morality, or – as Kant would say – with
practical reason (as distinguished from theoretical reason).
It is a matter of how subjective action and its representable
intentions relate to a universal Law. Ethics is the principle
that judges the practice of a Subject, be it individual or
collective.

Hegel will introduce a subtle distinction between 'ethics'
[*Sittlichkeit*] and 'morality' [*Moralität*]. He reserves the application of the ethical principle to *immediate* action, while
morality is to concern *reflexive* action. He will say, for
example, that 'the ethical order essentially consists in [the]
immediate firmness of decision'.[1]

The contemporary 'return to ethics' uses the word in an
obviously fuzzy way, but one that is certainly closer to Kant
(the ethics of judgement) than to Hegel (the ethics of
decision).

In fact, ethics designates today a principle that governs
how we relate to 'what is going on', a vague way of regulating
our commentary on historical situations (the ethics of
human rights), technico-scientific situations (medical ethics,
bio-ethics), 'social' situations (the ethics of being-together),
media situations (the ethics of communication), and so on.

This norm of commentaries and opinions is backed up
by official institutions, and carries its own authority: we now
have 'national ethical commissions', nominated by the
State. Every profession questions itself about its 'ethics'. We
even deploy military expeditions in the name of 'the ethics
of human rights'.

With respect to today's socially inflated recourse to ethics,
the purpose of this essay is twofold:

- To begin with, I will examine the precise nature of this phenomenon, which is the major 'philosophical' tendency of the day, as much in public opinion as for our official institutions. I will try to establish that in reality it amounts to a genuine nihilism, a threatening denial of thought as such.
- I will then argue against this meaning of the term 'ethics', and propose a very different one. Rather than link the word to abstract categories (Man or Human, Right or Law, the Other . . .), it should be referred back to particular *situations*. Rather than reduce it to an aspect of pity for victims, it should become the enduring maxim of *singular processes*. Rather than make of it merely the province of conservatism with a good conscience, it should concern the destiny of *truth*s, in the plural.

Note

1. G. W. F. Hegel, *The Phenomenology of Spirit*, para. 466, p. 280. The whole of this section of the *Phenomenology* is difficult, but very suggestive.

1

Does Man Exist?

According to the way it is generally used today, the term 'ethics' relates above all to the domain of human rights, 'the rights of man' – or, by derivation, the rights of living beings.

We are supposed to assume the existence of a universally recognizable human subject possessing 'rights' that are in some sense natural: the right to live, to avoid abusive treatment, to enjoy 'fundamental' liberties (of opinion, of expression, of democratic choice in the election of governments, etc.). These rights are held to be self-evident, and the result of a wide consensus. 'Ethics' is a matter of busying ourselves with these rights, of making sure that they are respected.

This return to the old doctrine of the natural rights of man is obviously linked to the collapse of revolutionary Marxism, and of all the forms of progressive engagement that it inspired. In the political domain, deprived of any collective political landmark, stripped of any notion of the 'meaning of History' and no longer able to hope for or expect a social revolution, many intellectuals, along with much of public opinion, have been won over to the logic of a capitalist economy and a parliamentary democracy. In the domain of 'philosophy', they have rediscovered the virtues of that ideology constantly defended by their former opponents: humanitarian individualism and the liberal defence of rights against the constraints imposed by organized political engagement. Rather than seek out the terms of a new politics of collective liberation, they have, in sum, adopted as their own the principles of the established 'Western' order.

In so doing, they have inspired a violently reactionary movement against all that was thought and proposed in the 1960s.

I The death of Man?

In those years, Michel Foucault outraged his readers with the declaration that Man, in the sense of constituent subject, was a constructed historical concept peculiar to a certain order of discourse, and not a timelessly self-evident principle capable of founding human rights or a universal ethics. He announced the end of this concept's relevance, once the kind of discourse which alone had made it meaningful became historically obsolete.

Likewise, Louis Althusser declared that history was not, as Hegel had thought, the absolute development [*devenir*] of Spirit, nor the advent of a subject-substance, but a rational, regulated process which he called a 'process without a subject', and which could be grasped only through a particular science, the science of historical materialism. It followed that the humanism of human rights and ethics in the abstract sense were merely imaginary constructions – ideologies – and that we should develop, rather, what he called a 'theoretical antihumanism'.

At the same time, Jacques Lacan strove to disentangle psychoanalysis from all its psychological and normative tendencies. He demonstrated how it was essential to distinguish the Ego, a figure of only imaginary unity, from the Subject. He showed that the subject had no substance, no 'nature', being a function both of the contingent laws of language and of the always singular history of objects of desire. It followed that any notion of analytic treatment as a means for the reinstatement of a 'normal' kind of desire was a fraud, and that, more generally, there existed no norm that could ground the idea of a 'human subject', a norm whose rights and duties it would have been the task of philosophy to articulate.

What was contested in this way was the idea of a natural or spiritual identity of Man, and with it, as a consequence, the very foundation of an 'ethical' doctrine in today's sense of the word: a consensual law-making concerning human beings in general, their needs, their lives, and their deaths – and, by extension, the self-evident, universal demarcation of evil, of what is incompatible with the human essence.

Is this to say, then, that Foucault, Althusser and Lacan extol an acceptance of the status quo, a kind of cynicism, an indifference to what people suffer? Thanks to a paradox which we will explain in what follows, the truth is *exactly the opposite*: all three were – each in his own way, and far more than those who uphold the cause of 'ethics' and 'human rights' today – the attentive and courageous militants of a cause. Michel Foucault, for example, maintained a particularly rigorous commitment [*engagement*] to a revision of the status of prisoners, and devoted to this question much of his time and the whole of his immense talent as an organizer and an agitator. Althusser's sole purpose was to redefine a genuinely emancipatory politics. Lacan himself – beyond the fact that he was a 'total' clinical analyst who spent the best part of his life listening to people – conceived of his struggle against the 'normative' orientation of American psychoanalysis, and the degrading subordination of thought to the 'American way of life',[1] as a decisive commitment [*engagement*]. For Lacan, questions of organization and polemic were always of a piece with questions of theory.

When those who uphold the contemporary ideology of 'ethics' tell us that the return to Man and his rights has delivered us from the 'fatal abstractions' inspired by 'the ideologies' of the past, they have some nerve. I would be delighted to see today so constant an attention paid to concrete situations, so sustained and so patient a concern for the real [*le réel*], so much time devoted to an activist inquiry into the situation of the most varied kinds of people – often the furthest removed, it might seem, from the normal environment of intellectuals – as that we witnessed in the years between 1965 and 1980.

In reality, there is no lack of proof for the fact that the thematics of the 'death of man' are compatible with rebellion, a radical dissatisfaction with the established order, and a fully committed engagement in the real of situations [*dans le réel des situations*], while by contrast, the theme of ethics and of human rights is compatible with the self-satisfied egoism of the affluent West, with advertising, and with service rendered to the powers that be. Such are the facts.

To elucidate these facts, we must examine the foundations of today's 'ethical' orientation.

II The foundations of the ethic of human rights

The explicit reference of this orientation, in the corpus of classical philosophy, is Kant.[2] Our contemporary moment is defined by an immense 'return to Kant'. In truth, the variety and the detail of this return are labyrinthine in their complexity; here I will concern myself only with the 'average' version of the doctrine.

What essentially is retained from Kant (or from an image of Kant, or, better still, from theorists of 'natural law') is the idea that there exist formally representable imperative demands that are to be subjected neither to empirical considerations nor to the examination of situations; that these imperatives apply to cases of offence, of crime, of Evil; that these imperatives must be punished by national and international law; that, as a result, governments are obliged to include them in their legislation, and to accept the full legal range of their implications; that if they do not, we are justified in forcing their compliance (the right to humanitarian interference, or to legal interference).

Ethics is conceived here both as an a priori ability to discern Evil (for according to the modern usage of ethics, Evil – or the negative – is primary: we presume a consensus regarding what is barbarian), and as the ultimate principle of judgement, in particular political judgement: good is what intervenes visibly against an Evil that is identifiable a priori. Law [*droit*] itself is first of all law 'against' Evil. If 'the rule of law' [*Etat de droit*] is obligatory, that is because it alone authorizes a space for the identification of Evil (this is the 'freedom of opinion' which, in the ethical vision, is first and foremost the freedom to designate Evil) and provides the means of arbitration when the issue is not clear (the apparatus of judicial precautions).

The presuppositions of this cluster of convictions are clear.

1. We posit a general human subject, such that whatever evil befalls him is universally identifiable (even if this universality often goes by the altogether paradoxical name of 'public opinion'), such that this subject is both, on the one hand, a passive, pathetic [*pathétique*], or reflexive subject – he who suffers – and, on the other, the active, determining subject of judgement – he who, in identifying suffering, knows that it must be stopped by all available means.

2. Politics is subordinated to ethics, to the single perspective that really matters in this conception of things: the sympathetic and indignant judgement of the spectator of the circumstances.

3. Evil is that from which the Good is derived, not the other way round.

4. 'Human rights' are rights to non-Evil: rights not to be offended or mistreated with respect to one's life (the horrors of murder and execution), one's body (the horrors of torture, cruelty and famine), or one's cultural identity (the horrors of the humiliation of women, of minorities, etc.).

The power of this doctrine rests, at first glance, in its self-evidence. Indeed, we know from experience that suffering is highly visible. The eighteenth-century theoreticians had already made pity – identification with the suffering of a living being – the mainspring of the relation with the other. That political leaders are discredited chiefly by their corruption, indifference or cruelty was a fact already noted by the Greek theorists of tyranny. That it is easier to establish consensus regarding what is evil rather than regarding what is good is a fact already established by the experience of the Church: it was always easier for church leaders to indicate what was forbidden – indeed, to content themselves with such abstinences – than to try to figure out what should be done. It is certainly true, moreover, that every politics worthy of the name finds its point of departure in the way people represent their lives and rights.

It might seem, then, that we have here a body of self-evident principles capable of cementing a global consensus, and of imposing themselves strongly.

Yet we must insist that it is not so; that this 'ethics' is inconsistent, and that the – perfectly obvious – reality of the situation is characterized in fact by the unrestrained pursuit of self-interest, the disappearance or extreme fragility of emancipatory politics, the multiplication of 'ethnic' conflicts, and the universality of unbridled competition.

III Man: Living animal or immortal singularity?

The heart of the question concerns the presumption of a universal human Subject, capable of reducing ethical issues to matters of human rights and humanitarian actions.

We have seen that ethics subordinates the identification of this subject to the universal recognition of the evil that is done to him. Ethics thus defines man *as a victim*. It will be objected: 'No! You are forgetting the active subject, the one that intervenes against barbarism!' So let us be precise: man is *the being who is capable of recognizing himself as a victim*.

It is this definition that we must proclaim unacceptable –
for three reasons in particular:

1. In the first place, because the status of victim, of
suffering beast, of emaciated, dying body, equates man with
his animal substructure, it reduces him to the level of a
living organism pure and simple (life being, as Bichat says,
nothing other than 'the set of functions that resist death').[3]
To be sure, humanity is an animal species. It is mortal and
predatory. But neither of these attributes can distinguish
humanity within the world of the living. In his role as
executioner, man is an animal abjection, but we must have
the courage to add that in his role as victim, he is generally
worth little more. The stories told by survivors of torture[4]
forcefully underline the point: if the torturers and bureau-
crats of the dungeons and the camps are able to treat their
victims like animals destined for the slaughterhouse, with
whom they themselves, the well-nourished criminals, have
nothing in common, it is because the victims have indeed
become such animals. What had to be done for this to
happen has indeed been done. That some nevertheless
remain human beings, and testify to that effect, is a confirmed fact. But this is always achieved precisely through
enormous effort, an effort acknowledged by witnesses (in
whom it excites a radiant recognition) as an almost incom-
prehensible resistance on the part of that which, in them,
does not coincide with the identity of victim. This is where we are
to find Man, if we are determined to *think* him [*le penser*]:
in what ensures, as Varlam Shalamov puts in his *Stories of
Life in the Camps,*[5] that we are dealing with an animal whose
resistance, unlike that of a horse, lies not in his fragile body
but in his stubborn determination to remain what he is

– that is to say, precisely something other than a victim, other than a being-for-death, and thus: *something other than a mortal being.*

An immortal: this is what the worst situations that can be inflicted upon Man show him to be, in so far as he distinguishes himself within the varied and rapacious flux of life. In order to think any aspect of Man, we must begin from this principle. So if 'rights of man' exist, they are surely not rights of life against death, or rights of survival against misery. They are the rights of the Immortal, affirmed in their own right, or the rights of the Infinite, exercised over the contingency of suffering and death. The fact that in the end we all die, that only dust remains, in no way alters Man's identity as immortal at the instant in which he affirms himself as someone who runs counter to the temptation of wanting-to-be-an-animal to which circumstances may expose him. And we know that every human being is *capable* of being this immortal – unpredictably, be it in circumstances great or small, for truths important or secondary. In each case, subjectivation is immortal, and makes Man. Beyond this there is only a biological species, a 'biped without feathers', whose charms are not obvious.

If we do not set out from this point (which can be summarized, very simply, as the assertion that Man *thinks*, that Man is a tissue of truths), if we equate Man with the simple reality of his living being, we are inevitably pushed to a conclusion quite opposite to the one that the principle of life seems to imply. For this 'living being' is in reality contemptible, and *he will indeed be held in contempt.* Who can fail to see that in our humanitarian expeditions, interventions, embarkations of charitable *légionnaires*, the Subject presumed to be universal is split? On the side of the victims, the haggard animal exposed on television screens. On the side of the benefactors, conscience and the imperative to intervene. And why does this splitting always assign the same roles to the same sides? Who cannot see that this ethics which rests on the misery of the world hides, behind its victim-Man, the good-Man, the white-Man? Since the barbarity of the situation is considered only in terms of 'human rights' – whereas in fact we are always dealing with a political situation, one that calls for a political thought-practice, one that is peopled by its own authentic actors – it is perceived, from the heights of our apparent civil peace, as the uncivilized that demands of the civilized a civilizing intervention. Every intervention in the name of a civilization *requires* an initial contempt for the situation as a whole, including its victims. And this is why the reign of 'ethics' coincides, after decades of courageous critiques of colonialism and imperialism, with today's sordid self-satisfaction in the 'West', with the insistent argument according to which the misery of the Third World is the result of its own incompetence, its own inanity – in short, of its *subhumanity*.

2. In the second place, because if the ethical 'consensus' is founded on the recognition of Evil, it follows that every effort to unite people around a positive idea of the Good, let alone to identify Man with projects of this kind, becomes in fact the real source of evil itself. Such is the accusation so often repeated over the last fifteen years: every revolutionary project stigmatized as 'utopian' turns, we are told, into totalitarian nightmare. Every will to inscribe an idea of justice or equality turns bad. Every collective will to the Good creates Evil.[6]

This is sophistry at its most devastating. For if our only agenda is an ethical engagement against an Evil we

recognize a priori, how are we to envisage any transformation of the way things are? From what source will man draw
the strength to be the immortal that he is? What shall be
the destiny of thought, since we know very well that it must
be affirmative invention or nothing at all? In reality, the
price paid by ethics is a stodgy conservatism. The ethical
conception of man, besides the fact that its foundation is
either biological (images of victims) or 'Western' (the self-
satisfaction of the armed benefactor), prohibits every broad,
positive vision of possibilities. What is vaunted here, what
ethics legitimates, is in fact the conservation by the so-called
'West' of what it possesses. It is squarely astride these
possessions (material possessions, but also possession of its
own being) that ethics determines Evil to be, in a certain
sense, simply that which it does not own and enjoy [*ce qui
n'est pas ce dont elle jouit*]. But Man, as immortal, is sustained
by the incalculable and the un-possessed. He is sustained by
non-being [*non-étant*]. To forbid him to imagine the Good,
to devote his collective powers to it, to work towards the
realization of unknown possibilities, to think what might be
in terms that break radically with what is, is quite simply to
forbid him humanity as such.

3. Finally, thanks to its negative and a priori determination of Evil, ethics prevents itself from thinking the singularity of situations as such, which is the obligatory starting
point of all properly human action. Thus, for instance, the
doctor won over to 'ethical' ideology will ponder, in meet-
ings and commissions, all sorts of considerations regarding
'the sick', conceived of in exactly the same way as the
partisan of human rights conceives of the indistinct crowd
of victims – the 'human' totality of subhuman entities [*réels*].
But the same doctor will have no difficulty in accepting the

fact that *this* particular person is not treated at the hospital, and accorded all necessary measures, because he or she is without legal residency papers, or not a contributor to Social Security. Once again, 'collective' responsibility demands it! What is erased in the process is the fact that there is only one medical situation, the clinical situation,[7] and there is no need for an 'ethics' (but only for a clear vision of *this* situation) to understand that in these circumstances a doctor is a doctor only if he deals with the situation according to the rule of maximum possibility – to treat this person who demands treatment of him (no intervention here!) as thoroughly as he can, using everything he knows and with all the means at his disposal, without taking anything else into consideration. And if he is to be prevented from giving treatment because of the State budget, because of death rates or laws governing immigration, then let them send for the police! Even so, his strict Hippocratic duty would oblige him to resist them, with force if necessary. 'Ethical commissions' and other ruminations on 'health-care expenses' or 'managerial responsibility', since they are radically exterior to the one situation that is genuinely medical, can in reality only prevent us from being *faithful* to it. For to be faithful to this situation means: to treat it *right to the limit* of the possible. Or, if you prefer: to draw from this situation, to the greatest possible extent, the affirmative humanity that it contains. Or again: to try to be the immortal of this situation.

As a matter of fact, bureaucratic medicine that complies with ethical ideology depends on 'the sick' conceived as vague victims or statistics, but is quickly overwhelmed by any urgent, singular situation of need. Hence the reduction of 'managed', 'responsible' and 'ethical' health-care to the

abject task of deciding which sick people the 'French medical system' can treat and which others – because the Budget
and public opinion demand it – it must send away to die in
the shantytowns of Kinshasa.

IV Some principles

We must reject the ideological framework of 'ethics', and
concede nothing to the negative and victimary definition of
man. This framework equates man with a simple mortal
animal, it is the symptom of a disturbing conservatism, and
– because of its abstract, statistical generality – it prevents
us from thinking the singularity of situations.

I will advance three opposing theses:

- Thesis 1: Man is to be identified by his affirmative
  thought, by the singular truths of which he is capable, by
  the Immortal which makes of him the most resilient
  [*résistant*] and most paradoxical of animals.
- Thesis 2: It is from our positive capability for Good, and
  thus from our boundary-breaking treatment of possibilities and our refusal of conservatism, including the
  conservation of being, that we are to identify Evil – not
  vice versa.
- Thesis 3: All humanity has its root in the identification in
  thought [*en pensée*] of singular situations. There is no
  ethics in general. There are only – eventually – ethics of
  processes by which we treat the possibilities of a situation.

At this point the refined man of ethics will object, murmur-
ing: 'Wrong! Wrong from the beginning. Ethics is in no

sense founded on the identity of the Subject, not even on his identity as recognized victim. From the beginning, ethics is the ethics of the other, it is the principal opening to the other, it subordinates identity to difference.'

Let us examine this line of argument. Does it contribute something new?

Notes

1. [In English in the original. *Translator's note.*]
2. Immanuel Kant, *Groundwork of the Metaphysics of Morals.*
3. Bichat was an eighteenth-century French doctor, anatomist and physiologist.
4. Henri Alleg, *La Question*, 1958. It is well worth referring to some of our own episodes of torture, systematically practised by the *French* army between 1954 and 1962.
5. Varlam Shalamov, *Kolyma Tales: Stories of Life in the Camps*, 1980 [1980]. This genuinely admirable book lends the form of art to a true ethics.
6. André Glucksmann, *The Master Thinkers*, 1977 [1980]. It is Glucksmann who has been most insistent on the absolute priority of the awareness of Evil, and on the idea that the catastrophic primacy [*primat*] of the Good was a creation of philosophy. 'Ethical' ideology is thus rooted, in part, in the work of the 'new philosophers' of the late 1970s.
7. See Cécile Winter, *Qu'en est-il de l'historicité actuelle de la clinique?* (inspired by an idea of Foucault's). This text demonstrates a most rigorous will to rethink medicine, in contemporary conditions, in such a way that it recognizes clinical requirements as its sole concern.

2

Does the Other Exist?

The conception of ethics as the 'ethics of the other' or the 'ethics of difference' has its origin in the theses of Emmanuel Lévinas rather than in those of Kant.

Lévinas has devoted his work, after a brush with phenomenology (an exemplary confrontation between Husserl and Heidegger), to the deposing [*destitution*] of philosophy in favour of ethics. It is to him that we owe, long before the current fashion, a kind of ethical radicalism.[1]

I Ethics according to Lévinas

Roughly speaking: Lévinas maintains that metaphysics, imprisoned by its Greek origins, has subordinated thought to the logic of the Same, to the primacy of substance and identity. But, according to Lévinas, it is impossible to arrive at an authentic thought of the Other (and thus an ethics of the relation to the Other) from the despotism of the Same, which is incapable of recognizing this Other. The dialectic of the Same and the Other, conceived 'ontologically' under the dominance of self-identity [*identité-à-soi*], ensures the absence of the Other in effective thought, suppresses all genuine experience of the Other, and bars the way to an ethical opening to alterity. So we must push thought over to a different origin, a non-Greek origin, one that proposes a radical, primary opening to the Other conceived as ontologically anterior to the construction of identity. It is in the Jewish tradition that Lévinas finds the basis for this pushing over. What the Law (understood according to Jewish tradition as both immemorial and currently in effect) names is precisely the anteriority, founded in being-before-the-Same, and with respect to theoretical thought, of the ethics of the relation to the Other, itself conceived merely as the 'objective' identification of regularities and identities. The Law, indeed, does not tell me what is, but what is imposed by the existence of others. This Law (of the Other) might be opposed to the laws (of the real).

According to Greek thought, adequate action presumes an initial theoretical mastery of experience, which ensures that the action is in conformity with the rationality of being. From this point of departure are deduced laws (in the plural) of the City and of action. According to Jewish ethics, in Lévinas's sense, everything is grounded in the immediacy of an opening to the Other which disarms the reflexive subject. The 'thou [*tu*]' prevails over the 'I'. Such is the whole meaning of *the* Law.

Lévinas proposes a whole series of phenomenological themes for testing and exploring the originality of the Other, at the centre of which lies the theme of the face, of the singular giving [*donation*] of the Other 'in person', through his fleshly epiphany, which does not test mimetic recognition (the Other as 'similar', *identical* to me), but, on the contrary, is that from which I experience myself ethically as 'pledged' to the appearing of the Other, and subordinated in my being to this pledge.

For Lévinas, ethics is *the new name of thought*, thought which has thrown off its 'logical' chains (the principle of identity) in favour of its prophetic submission to the Law of founding alterity.

II The 'ethics of difference'

Whether they know it or not, it is in the name of this configuration that the proponents of ethics explain to us today that it amounts to 'recognition of the other' (against racism, which would deny this other), or to 'the ethics of differences' (against substantialist nationalism, which would exclude immigrants, or sexism, which would deny feminine-being), or to 'multiculturalism' (against the imposition of a unified model of behaviour and intellectual approach). Or, quite simply, to good old-fashioned 'tolerance', which consists of not being offended by the fact that others think and act differently from you.

This commonsensical discourse has neither force nor truth. It is defeated in advance in the competition it declares between 'tolerance' and 'fanaticism', between 'the ethics of difference' and 'racism', between 'recognition of the other' and 'identitarian' fixity.

For the honour of philosophy, it is first of all necessary to admit that this ideology of a 'right to difference', the contemporary catechism of goodwill with regard to 'other cultures', are strikingly distant from Lévinas's actual conception of things.

III From the Other to the Altogether-Other

The principal – but also fairly superficial – objection that we might make to ethics in Lévinas's sense is: what is it that testifies to the originality of my de-votion [*dé-voue-ment*] to the Other? The phenomenological analyses of the face, of the caress, of love, cannot by themselves ground the anti-ontological (or anti-identitarian) thesis of the author of *Totality and Infinity*. A 'mimetic' conception that locates original access to the other in my own redoubled image also sheds light on that element of self-forgetting that characterizes the grasping of this other: what I cherish is that me-myself-at-a-distance which, precisely because it is 'objectified' for my consciousness, founds me as a stable construction, as an interiority accessible *in its exteriority*. Psychoanalysis explains brilliantly how this construction of the Ego in the identification with the other – this mirror-effect[2] – combines narcissism (I delight in the exteriority of the other in so far as he figures as myself made visible to myself) and aggressivity (I invest in the other my death drive, my own archaic desire for self-destruction).

Here, however, we are a very long way from what Lévinas wants to tell us. As always, the pure analysis of phenomenal appearing cannot decide between divergent orientations of thought.

We need, in addition, to make explicit the axioms of thought that *decide* an orientation.

The difficulty, which also defines the point of application for these axioms, can be explained as follows: the ethical primacy of the Other over the Same requires that the experience of alterity be ontologically 'guaranteed' as the experience of a distance, or of an essential non-identity, the *traversal* of which is the ethical experience itself. But nothing in the simple phenomenon of the other contains such a guarantee. And this simply because the finitude of the other's appearing certainly *can* be conceived as resemblance, or as imitation, and thus lead back to the logic of the Same. The other always resembles me too much for the hypothesis of an originary exposure to his alterity to be *necessarily* true.

The phenomenon of the other (his face) must then attest to a radical alterity which he nevertheless does not contain by himself. The Other, as he appears to me in the order of the finite, must be the epiphany of a properly infinite distance to the other, the traversal of which is the originary ethical experience.

This means that in order to be intelligible, ethics requires that the Other be in some sense *carried by a principle of alterity* which transcends mere finite experience. Lévinas calls this principle the 'Altogether-Other', and it is quite obviously the ethical name for God. There can be no Other if he is not the immediate phenomenon of the Altogether-Other. There can be no finite devotion to the non-identical if it is not sustained by the infinite devotion of the principle to that which subsists outside it. There can be no ethics without God the ineffable.

In Lévinas's enterprise, the ethical dominance of the Other over the theoretical ontology of the same is entirely bound up with a religious axiom; to believe that we can separate what Lévinas's thought unites is to betray the intimate movement of this thought, its subjective rigour. In truth, Lévinas has no philosophy – not even philosophy as the 'servant' of theology. Rather, this is philosophy (in the Greek sense of the word) *annulled* by theology, itself no longer a theology (the terminology is still too Greek, and presumes proximity to the divine via the identity and predicates of God) but, precisely, an ethics.

To make of ethics the ultimate name of the religious as such (i.e. of that which relates [*re-lie*] to the Other under the ineffable authority of the Altogether-Other) is to distance it still more completely from all that can be gathered under the name of 'philosophy'.

To put it crudely: Lévinas's enterprise serves to remind us, with extraordinary insistence, that every effort to turn ethics into the principle of thought and action is essentially religious. We might say that Lévinas is the coherent and inventive thinker of an assumption that no academic exercise of veiling or abstraction can obscure: distanced from its Greek usage (according to which it is clearly subordinated to the theoretical), and taken in general, ethics is a category of pious discourse.

IV Ethics as decomposed [*décomposée*] religion

What then becomes of this category if we claim to suppress, or mask, its religious character, all the while preserving the abstract arrangement of its apparent constitution ('recognition of the other', etc.)? The answer is obvious: a dog's dinner [*de la bouillie pour les chats*]. We are left with a pious discourse without piety, a spiritual supplement for incompetent governments, and a cultural sociology preached, in line with the new-style sermons, in lieu of the late class struggle.

Our suspicions are first aroused when we see that the self-declared apostles of ethics and of the 'right to difference' are clearly *horrified by any vigorously sustained difference.* For them, African customs are barbaric, Muslims are dreadful, the Chinese are totalitarian, and so on. As a matter of fact, this celebrated 'other' is acceptable only if he is a *good* other – which is to say what, exactly, if not *the same as us?* Respect for differences, of course! But on condition that the different be parliamentary-democratic, pro free-market economics, in favour of freedom of opinion, feminism, the environment. . . . That is to say: I respect differences, but only, of course, in so far as that which differs also respects, just as I do, the said differences. Just as there can be 'no freedom for the enemies of freedom', so there can be no respect for those whose difference consists precisely in not respecting differences. To prove the point, just consider the obsessive resentment expressed by the partisans of ethics regarding anything that resembles an Islamic 'fundamentalist'.

The problem is that the 'respect for differences' and the ethics of human rights do seem to define an *identity*! And that as a result, the respect for differences applies only to those differences that are reasonably consistent with this identity (which, after all, is nothing other than the identity of a wealthy – albeit visibly declining – 'West'). Even immigrants in this country [France], as seen by the partisans of ethics, are acceptably different only when they are 'integrated', only if they seek integration (which seems to mean, if you think about it: only if they want to *suppress* their difference). It might well be that ethical ideology, detached from the religious teachings which at least conferred upon it the fullness of a 'revealed' identity, is simply the final imperative of a conquering civilization: 'Become like me and I will respect your difference.'

V Return to the Same

The truth is that, in the context of a system of thought that is both a-religious and genuinely contemporary with the truths of our time, the whole ethical predication based upon recognition of the other should be purely and simply abandoned. For the real question – and it is an extraordinarily difficult one – is much more that of *recognizing the Same*.

Let us posit *our* axioms. There is no God. Which also means: the One is not. The multiple 'without-one' – every multiple being in its turn nothing other than a multiple of multiples – is the law of being. The only stopping point is the void. The infinite, as Pascal had already realized, is the banal reality of every situation, not the predicate of a transcendence. For the infinite, as Cantor demonstrated with the creation of set theory, is actually only the most general form of multiple-being [*être-multiple*]. In fact, every situation, inasmuch as it is, is a multiple composed of an infinity of elements, each one of which is itself a multiple. Considered in their simple belonging to a situation (to an infinite multiple), the animals of the species *Homo sapiens* are ordinary multiplicities.

What, then, are we to make of the other, of differences, and of their ethical recognition?

Infinite alterity is quite simply *what there is*. Any experience at all is the infinite deployment of infinite differences. Even the apparently reflexive experience of myself is by no

means the intuition of a unity but a labyrinth of differentia-
tions, and Rimbaud was certainly not wrong when he said:
'I am another.' There are as many differences, say, between
a Chinese peasant and a young Norwegian professional as
between myself and anybody at all, including myself.

As many, but also, then, *neither more nor less.*

VI 'Cultural' differences and culturalism

Contemporary ethics kicks up a big fuss about 'cultural'
differences. Its conception of the 'other' is informed mainly
by this kind of differences. Its great ideal is the peaceful
coexistence of cultural, religious, and national 'communities', the refusal of 'exclusion'.

But what we must recognize is that these differences hold
no interest for thought, that they amount to nothing more
than the infinite and self-evident multiplicity of human-
kind, as obvious in the difference between me and my
cousin from Lyon as it is between the Shi'ite 'community'
of Iraq and the fat cowboys of Texas.

The objective (or historical) foundation of contemporary
ethics is culturalism, in truth a tourist's fascination for the
diversity of morals, customs and beliefs. And in particular,
for the irreducible medley of imaginary formations (religions, sexual representations, incarnations of authority . . .).
Yes, the essential 'objective' basis of ethics rests on a vulgar
sociology, directly inherited from the astonishment of the
colonial encounter with savages. And we must not forget
that there are also savages among us (the drug addicts of
the *banlieues*, religious sects – the whole journalistic para-
phernalia of menacing internal alterity), confronted by an

ethics that offers, without changing its means of investigation, *its* 'recognition' and *its* social workers.

Against these trifling descriptions (of a reality that is both obvious and inconsistent in itself), genuine thought should affirm the following principle: since differences are what there is, and since every truth is the coming-to-be of that which is not yet, so differences are then precisely what truths depose, or render insignificant. No light is shed on any concrete situation by the notion of the 'recognition of the other'. Every modern collective configuration involves people from everywhere, who have their different ways of eating and speaking, who wear different sorts of headgear, follow different religions, have complex and varied relations to sexuality, prefer authority or disorder, and such is the way of the world.

VII From the Same to truths

Philosophically, if the other doesn't matter it is indeed because the difficulty lies on the side of the Same. The Same, in effect, is not what is (i.e. the infinite multiplicity of differences) but what *comes to be*. I have already named that in regard to which only the advent of the Same occurs: it is a *truth*. Only a truth is, as such, *indifferent to differences*. This is something we have always known, even if sophists of every age have always attempted to obscure its certainty: a truth is *the same for all*.

What is to be postulated for one and all, what I have called our 'being immortal', certainly is not covered by the logic of 'cultural' differences as insignificant as they are massive. It is our capacity for truth – our capacity to be that

'*same*' *that a truth convokes to its own* '*sameness*'. Or in other
words, depending on the circumstances, our capacity for
science, love, politics or art, since all truths, in my view, fall
under one or another of these universal names.

It is only through a genuine perversion, for which we will
pay a terrible historical price, that we have sought to
elaborate an 'ethics' on the basis of cultural relativism. For
this is to pretend that a merely contingent state of things
can found a Law.

The only genuine ethics is of truths in the plural – or,
more precisely, the only ethics is of processes of truth, of
the labour that brings *some* truths into the world. Ethics
must be taken in the sense presumed by Lacan when,
against Kant and the notion of a general morality, he
discusses the ethics *of* psychoanalysis. Ethics does not exist.
There is only the *ethic-of* (of politics, of love, of science, of
art).

There is not, in fact, one single Subject, but as many
subjects as there are truths, and as many subjective types as
there are procedures of truths.

As for me, I identify four fundamental subjective 'types':
political, scientific, artistic, and amorous [*amoureux*].

Every human animal, by participating in a given singular
truth, is inscribed in one of these four types.

A philosophy sets out to construct a *space of thought* in
which the different subjective types, expressed by the singular truths of its time, coexist. But this coexistence is not a
unification – that is why it is impossible to speak of *one*
Ethics.

Notes

1. Emmanuel Lévinas, *Totality and Infinity*, 1961 [1969]. This is his major work.
2. Jacques Lacan, 'The Mirror Phase', in *Ecrits: A Selection*, 1966 [1977].

3

Ethics as a Figure of Nihilism

Whether we think of it as the consensual representation of Evil or as concern for the other, ethics designates above all the incapacity, so typical of the contemporary world, to name and strive for a Good. We should go even further, and say that the reign of ethics is one symptom of a universe ruled by a distinctive [*singulière*] combination of resignation in the face of necessity together with a purely negative, if not destructive, will. It is this combination that should be designated as nihilism.

Nietzsche demonstrated very neatly that humanity prefers to will nothingness rather than to will nothing at all. I will reserve the name nihilism for this will to nothingness, which is like a kind of understudy [*doublure*] of blind necessity.

I Ethics as the servant of necessity

The modern name for necessity is, as everyone knows, 'economics'. Economic objectivity – which should be called by its name: the logic of Capital – is the basis from which our parliamentary regimes organize a subjectivity and a public opinion condemned in advance to ratify what seems necessary. Unemployment, the anarchy of production, inequalities, the complete devaluation of manual work, the persecution of foreigners: all this fits together as part of a debased consensus regarding a state of things as changeable as the weather (the predictions of economic 'science' being still more uncertain than those of meteorology), yet apparently shaped by inflexible and interminable external constraint.

Parliamentary politics as practised today does not in any way consist of setting objectives inspired by principles and of inventing the means to attain them. It consists of turning the spectacle of the economy into the object of an apathetic (though obviously unstable) public consensus. In itself, the economy is neither good nor bad; it is the place of no value (other than commercial value, and of money as general form of equivalence). It simply 'runs' more or less well. Routine politics is the subjective or valorizing moment of this neutral exteriority. For the possibilities whose development it pretends to organize are in reality circumscribed and annulled, in advance, by the external neutrality of the economic referent – in such a way that subjectivity in general is inevitably dragged down into a kind of belligerent impotence, the emptiness of which is filled by elections and the 'sound-bites' of party leaders.

Right from the first moment in the constitution of contemporary subjectivity (as 'public opinion'), ethics has duly played its accompanying role. For from the beginning it confirms the absence of any project, of any emancipatory politics, or any genuinely collective cause. By blocking, in the name of Evil and of human rights, the way towards the positive prescription of possibilities, the way towards the

Good as the superhumanity of humanity, towards the Immortal as the master of time, it accepts the play of necessity as the objective basis for all judgements of value.

The celebrated 'end of ideologies' heralded everywhere as the good news which opens the way for the 'return of ethics' signifies in fact an espousal of the twistings and turnings of necessity, and an extraordinary impoverishment of the active, militant value of principles.

The very idea of a consensual 'ethics', stemming from the general feeling provoked by the sight of atrocities, which replaces the 'old ideological divisions', is a powerful contributor to subjective resignation and acceptance of the status quo. For what every emancipatory project does, what every emergence of hitherto unknown possibilities does, is to put an end to consensus. How, indeed, could the incalculable novelty of a truth, and the hole that it bores in established knowledges, be inscribed in a situation without encountering resolute opposition? Precisely because a truth, in its invention, is the only thing that is *for all*, so it can actually be achieved only *against* dominant opinions, since these always work for the benefit of some rather than all. These privileged few certainly benefit from their position, their capital, their control of the media, and so on. But in particular, they wield the inert power of reality and time [*de la réalité et du temps*] against that which is only, like every truth, the hazardous, precarious advent of a possibility of the Intemporal. As Mao Tse-tung used to say, with his customary simplicity: 'If you have an idea, one will have to split into two.' Yet ethics explicitly presents itself as the spiritual supplement of the consensus. The 'splitting into two' horrifies it (it smacks of ideology, it's *passé*...). Ethics is thus part of what prohibits any idea, any coherent project of thought, settling instead for overlaying unthought and anonymous situations with mere humanitarian prattle (which, as we have said, does not itself contain any positive idea of humanity).

And in the same way, the 'concern for the other' signifies that it is not a matter – that it is never a matter – of prescribing hitherto unexplored possibilities for *our* situation, and ultimately for ourselves. The Law (human rights, etc.) is always *already there*. It regulates judgements and opinions concerning the evil that happens in some variable elsewhere. But there is no question of reconsidering the foundation of this 'Law', of going right back to the conservative identity that sustains it.

As everyone knows, France – which, under Vichy, approved a law regulating the status of the Jews, and which at this very moment is voting to approve laws for the racial identification of an alleged internal enemy that goes by the name of 'illegal immigrant' [*immigré clandestin*]; France – which is subjectively dominated by fear and impotence – is an 'island of law and liberty'. Ethics is the ideology of this insularity, and this is why it valorizes – throughout the world, and with the complacency of 'intervention' – the gunboats of Law. But by doing this, by everywhere promoting a *domestic* haughtiness and cowardly self-satisfaction, it sterilizes every collective gathering around a vigorous conception [*pensée*] of what can (and thus must) be done *here and now*. And in this, once again, it is nothing more than a variant of the conservative consensus.

But what must be understood is that this resignation in the face of (economic) necessities is neither the only nor the worst component of the public spirit held together by ethics. For Nietzsche's maxim forces us to consider that every non-willing (every impotence) is shaped by a will to nothingness, whose other name is: death drive.

II Ethics as the 'Western' mastery of death

We should be more struck than we usually are by a remark that often recurs in articles and commentaries devoted to the war in the former Yugoslavia: it is pointed out – with a kind of subjective excitement, an ornamental pathos – that these atrocities are taking place 'only two hours by plane from Paris'. The authors of these texts invoke, naturally, all the 'rights of man', ethics, humanitarian intervention, the fact that Evil (thought to have been exorcized by the collapse of 'totalitarianisms') is making a terrible comeback. But then the observation seems ludicrous: if it is a matter of ethical principles, of the victimary essence of Man, of the fact that 'rights are universal and imprescriptible', why should we care about the length of the flight? Is the 'recognition of the other' all the more intense if this other is in some sense almost within my reach?

In this *pathos* of proximity, we can almost sense the trembling equivocation, halfway between fear and enjoyment, of finally perceiving *so close to us* horror and destruction, war and cynicism. Here ethical ideology has at its disposal, almost knocking on the protected gates of civilized shelter, the revolting yet delicious combination of a complex Other (Croats, Serbs, and those enigmatic 'Muslims' of Bosnia) and an avowed Evil. History has delivered the ethical *dish* to our very door.

Ethics feeds too much on Evil and the Other not to take silent pleasure in seeing them close up (in a silence that is the abject underside of its prattle). For at the core of the mastery internal to ethics is always the power to decide who dies and who does not.

Ethics is nihilist because its underlying conviction is that the only thing that can really happen to someone is death. And it is certainly true *that in so far* as we deny truths, we thereby challenge the immortal disjunction that they effect in any given situation. Between Man as the possible basis for the uncertainty [*aléa*] of truths, or Man as being-for-death (or being-for-happiness, it is the same thing), you have to choose. It is the same choice that divides philosophy from 'ethics', or the courage of truths from nihilism.

III Bio-ethics

This, no doubt, is what explains the privilege that ethics grants, among the 'social issues' that spice up our daily routine – and all the more so, in that none of them makes the slightest sense – to the never-ending debate on euthanasia.

The word *euthanasia* poses the question very clearly: 'When and how, in the name of our idea of happiness, may we kill someone?' It names the stable core on which ethical sentiment depends. We all know the constant reference ethical 'thought' makes to 'human dignity'. And the combination of being-for-death and dignity constructs precisely the idea of a 'dignified death'.

Commissions, reporters, judges, politicians, priests, doctors, debate the ethical definition, sanctioned by law, of a death *administered* with dignity.

To be sure, suffering and degeneration are not 'dignified',

do not conform to the smooth, young, well-nourished image
that we have of Man and his rights. Who can fail to see that
the 'debate' on euthanasia points above all to the radical
poverty of the symbols available today for old age and
death? To the unbearable character of the latter as a sight
for the living? Here ethics is at the junction of two only
apparently contradictory drives: since it defines Man by
non-Evil, and thus by 'happiness' and life, it is simultaneously fascinated by death yet incapable of inscribing it
in thought. The upshot of this compromise is the transformation of death itself into a spectacle made as discreet as
possible, a mere disappearing, regarding which the living
have the right to hope that it will not disrupt their delu-
sional habits of contented ignorance. Ethical discourse is
thus both fatalist and resolutely non-tragic: it allows death
to 'go about its business', without opposing to it the Immortal of a resistance.

Let us remember – since such are the facts – that 'bio-
ethics' and the State's obsession with euthanasia were
explicit categories of Nazism. Fundamentally, Nazism was a
thoroughgoing ethics of Life. It had its own concept of
'dignified life', and it accepted, implacably, the necessity of
putting an end to undignified lives. Nazism isolated and
carried to its ultimate conclusion the nihilist core of the
'ethical' disposition once it has at its disposal the political
means to be something other than prattle. In this respect,
the appearance in our country of major state commissions
on 'bio-ethics' bodes ill. Here there will be loud cries of
protest. It will be said that it is precisely because of Nazism
that it is necessary to lay down the law protecting the right
to life and to dignity, once the impetuous advances of
science give us the means to practise all sorts of genetic

manipulations. We should not be impressed by these cries. We should argue strongly that the necessity of such state commissions and such laws indicates that, in the configuration of public and private minds, the whole problematic remains essentially suspect. The conjunction of 'ethics' and 'bio' is *in itself* threatening. So is the similarity of prefixes between (evil) *eu*genics and (respectable) *eu*thanasia. A hedonistic doctrine of 'dying-well' will make for no defence against the powerful and genuinely murderous aspiration of 'generating-well', an obvious component of 'living-well'.

The root of the problem is that, in a certain way, every definition of Man based on happiness is nihilist. It is clear that the external barricades erected to protect our sickly prosperity have as their internal counterpart, against the nihilist drive, the derisory and complicit barrier of ethical commissions.

When a prime minister,[1] the political eulogist of a civic ethics, declares that France 'cannot welcome [*accueillir*] all the misery of the world', he is careful not to tell us about the criteria and the methods that will allow us to distinguish the part of the said misery that we welcome from that part which we will request – no doubt from within detention centres – to return to its place of death, so that we might continue to enjoy those unshared riches which, as we know, condition both our happiness and our 'ethics'. And in the same way, it is certainly impossible to settle on stable, 'responsible', and of course 'collective' criteria in the name of which commissions on bio-ethics will distinguish between eugenics and euthanasia, between the scientific improvement of the white man and his happiness, and the elimination 'with dignity' of monsters, of those who suffer or become unpleasant to behold.

Chance, the circumstances of life, the tangle of beliefs, combined with the rigorous and impartial treatment without exception of the clinical situation, is worth a thousand times more than the pompous, made-for-media conscription of bio-ethical authorities [*instances*] – a conscription whose place of work, whose very name, have a nasty smell about them.

IV Ethical nihilism between conservatism and the death drive

Considered as a figure of nihilism, reinforced by the fact that our societies are without a future that can be presented as universal, ethics oscillates between two complementary desires: a conservative desire, seeking global recognition for the legitimacy of the order peculiar to our 'Western' position – the interweaving of an unbridled and impassive economy [*économie objective sauvage*] with a discourse of law; and a murderous desire that promotes and shrouds, in one and the same gesture, an integral mastery of life – or again, that dooms *what is* to the 'Western' mastery of death.

This is why ethics would be better named – since it speaks Greek – a '*eu-oudénose*', a smug nihilism.

Against this we can set only that which is not yet in being, but which our thought declares itself able to conceive.

Every age – and in the end, none is worth more than any other – has its own figure of nihilism. The names change, but always under these names ('ethics', for example) we find the articulation of conservative propaganda with an obscure desire for catastrophe.

It is only by declaring that we want what conservatism

decrees to be impossible, and by affirming truths against
the desire for nothingness, that we tear ourselves away from
nihilism. The possibility of the impossible, which is exposed
by every loving encounter, every scientific re-foundation,
every artistic invention and every sequence of emancipatory
politics, is the sole principle – against the ethics of living-
well whose real content is the deciding of death – of an
ethic of truths.

Note

1. [Badiou is referring to Michel Rocard. *Translator's note.*]

4

The Ethic of Truths

It is a difficult task, for the philosopher, to pull names away from a usage that prostitutes them. Already Plato had to take all possible pains to hold his ground with the word *justice*, against the sophist's quibbling and devious usage.

Let us nevertheless try to preserve this word *ethics*, in spite of all that has preceded this chapter, since those who, after Aristotle, have used the word in a reasonable way make up a long and honourable lineage.

I Being, event, truth, subject

If there is no ethics 'in general', that is because there is no abstract Subject, who would adopt it as his shield. There is only a particular kind of animal, convoked by certain circumstances to *become* a subject – or rather, to enter into the composing of a subject. This is to say that at a given moment, everything he is – his body, his abilities – is called upon to enable the passing of a truth along its path. This is when the human animal is convoked [*requis*] to be the immortal that he was not yet.

What are these 'circumstances'? They are the circumstances of a truth. But what are we to understand by that? It is clear that *what there is* [*ce qu'il y a*] (multiples, infinite differences, 'objective' situations – for example, the ordinary state of relation to the other, before a loving encounter) cannot define such a circumstance. In this kind of objectivity, every animal gets by as best it can. We must suppose, then, that whatever convokes someone to the composition of a subject is something extra, something that happens in situations as something that they and the usual way of behaving in them cannot account for. Let us say that a *subject*, which goes beyond the animal (although the animal remains its sole foundation [*support*]) needs something to have happened, something that cannot be reduced to its ordinary inscription in 'what there is'. Let us call this *supplement* an *event*, and let us distinguish multiple-being, where it is not a matter of truth (but only of opinions), from the event, which compels us to decide a *new* way of being.[1] Such events are well and truly attested: the French Revolution of 1792, the meeting of Héloïse and Abélard, Galileo's creation of physics, Haydn's invention of the classical musical style. . . . But also: the Cultural Revolution in China (1965–67), a personal amorous passion, the creation of Topos theory by the mathematician Grothendieck, the invention of the twelve-tone scale by Schoenberg. . . .

From which 'decision', then, stems the process of a truth? From the decision to relate henceforth to the situation *from the perspective of its evental [événementiel] supplement*. Let us call this a fidelity. To be faithful to an event is to move within the situation that this event has supplemented, by *thinking* (although all thought is a practice, a putting to the test) the situation 'according to' the event. And this, of course – since the event was excluded by all the regular laws of the situation – compels the subject to *invent* a new way of being and acting in the situation.

It is clear that under the effect of a loving encounter, if I want to be *really* faithful to it, I must completely rework my ordinary way of 'living' my situation. If I want to be faithful to the event of the 'Cultural Revolution', then I must at least practise politics (in particular the relation with the workers) in an entirely different manner from that proposed by the socialist and trade-unionist traditions. And again, Berg and Webern, faithful to the musical event known by the name of 'Schoenberg', cannot continue with *fin-de-siècle* neo-Romanticism as if nothing had happened. After Einstein's texts of 1905, if I am faithful to their radical novelty, I cannot continue to practise physics within its classical framework, and so on. An evental fidelity is a real break (both thought and practised) in the specific order within which the event took place (be it political, loving, artistic or scientific . . .).

I shall call 'truth' (*a* truth) the real process of a fidelity to an event: that which this fidelity *produces* in the situation. For example, the politics of the French Maoists between 1966 and 1976, which tried to think and practise a fidelity to two entangled events: the Cultural Revolution in China, and May '68 in France. Or so-called 'contemporary' music (a name as ubiquitous as it is strange), which is fidelity to the great Viennese composers of the early twentieth century. Or the algebraic geometry of the 1950s and 1960s, faithful to the concept of a Universe (in Grothendieck's sense of the term), and so forth. Essentially, a truth is the material course traced, within the situation, by the evental supplementation. It is thus an *immanent break*. 'Immanent' because a truth proceeds *in* the situation, and nowhere else

– there is no heaven of truths. 'Break' because what enables the truth-process – the event – meant nothing according to the prevailing language and established knowledge of the situation.

We might say, then, that a truth-process is heterogeneous to the instituted knowledges of the situation. Or – to use an expression of Lacan's – that it punches a 'hole [*trouée*]' in these knowledges.

I call 'subject' the bearer [*le support*] of a fidelity, the one who bears a process of truth. The subject, therefore, in no way pre-exists the process. He is absolutely nonexistent in the situation 'before' the event. We might say that the process of truth *induces* a subject.

It is important to understand that the 'subject', thus conceived, does not overlap with the psychological subject, nor even with the reflexive subject (in Descartes's sense) or the transcendental subject (in Kant's sense). For example, the subject induced by fidelity to an amorous encounter, the subject of love, is *not* the 'loving' subject described by the classical moralists. For this kind of psychological subject falls within the province of human nature, within the logic of passion, whereas what I am talking about has no 'natural' pre-existence. The lovers as such enter into the composition of *one* loving subject, who *exceeds* them both.

In the same way, the subject of a revolutionary politics is not the individual militant – any more, by the way, than it is the chimera of a class-subject. It is a singular production, which has taken different names (sometimes 'Party', sometimes not). To be sure, the militant enters into the composition of this subject, but once again it exceeds him (it is precisely this excess that makes it come to pass as immortal).

Or again, the subject of an artistic process is not the artist (the 'genius', etc.). In fact, the subject-points of art are works of art. And the artist enters into the composition of these subjects (the works are 'his'), without our being able in any sense to reduce them to 'him' (and besides, which 'him' would this be?).

Events are irreducible singularities, the 'beyond-the-law' of situations. Each faithful truth-process is an entirely invented immanent break with the situation. Subjects, which are the local occurrences of the truth-process ('points' of truth), are particular and incomparable inductions.

It is with respect to subjects of this kind that it is – perhaps – legitimate to speak of an 'ethic of truths'.

II Formal definition of the ethic of a truth

What I will call, in general, the 'ethic of a truth' is the principle that enables the continuation of a truth-process – or, to be more precise and complex, *that which lends consistency to the presence of some-one in the composition of the subject induced by the process of this truth.*

Let us unpack this formula.

1. What is to be understood by 'some-one'? 'Some-one' is an animal of the human species, this kind of particular multiple that established knowledges designate as belonging to the species. It is *this* body, and everything that it is capable of, which enters into the composition of a 'point of truth' – always assuming that an event has

occurred, along with an *immanent* break taking the *sustained* form of a *faithful* process.

'Some-one' can thus be *this* spectator whose thinking has been set in motion, who has been seized and bewildered by a burst of theatrical fire, and who thus enters into the complex configuration of a moment of art. Or this assiduous student of a mathematical problem, after the thankless and exhausting confusion of working in the dark, at the precise moment enlightened by its solution. Or that lover whose vision of reality is befuddled and displaced since, supported by the other, he remembers the instant of the declaration of their love. Or this militant who manages, at the end of a complicated meeting, to find simple words to express the hitherto elusive statement which, everyone agrees, declares what must be pursued in the situation.

The 'some-one' thus caught up in what attests that he belongs to the truth-process as one of its foundation-points is simultaneously *himself*, nothing other than himself, a multiple singularity recognizable among all others, and *in excess of himself*, because the uncertain course [*tracé aléatoire*] of fidelity *passes through him*, transfixes his singular body and inscribes him, from within time, in an instant of eternity.

Let us say that what we can know of him is entirely engaged in what took place, that there is, materially, nothing other than this referent of a knowledge, but that all this is taken up in the immanent break of a truth-process, such that, belonging both to his own situation (political, scientific, artistic, amorous . . .) and to the truth that *becomes*, 'some-one' is internally and imperceptibly *riven*, or punctured, by this truth that 'passes' through that *known* multiple that he is.

We might say, more simply: the 'some-one' was not in a position *to know that he was capable of* this co-belonging to a situation and to the hazardous course [*tracé hasardeux*] of a truth, this becoming-subject.

In so far as he enters into the composition of a subject, in so far as he is self-subjectivization, the 'some-one' exists *without knowing it* [*existe à son propre insu*].

2. What should we understand now by 'consistency'? Simply, that there is a *law of the not-known* [*de l'insu*]. For if the 'some-one' enters into the composition of a subject of truth only by exposing himself 'entirely' to a post-evental fidelity, then there remains the problem of knowing what he, this 'some-one', will *become* through this testing experience.

The ordinary behaviour of the human animal is a matter of what Spinoza calls 'perseverance in being', which is nothing other than the pursuit of interest, or the conservation of self. This perseverance is the law that governs some-one in so far as he knows himself. But the test of truth does not fall under this law. To belong to the situation is everyone's natural destiny, but to belong to the composition of a subject of truth concerns a particular route, a sustained break, and it is very difficult to know how this composition is to be superimposed upon or combined with the simple perseverance-of-self.

I shall call 'consistency' (or 'subjective consistency') the principle of this superimposition, or this combination. That is to say, the manner in which our devotee of mathematics will engage his perseverance in that which breaks or opposes this perseverance, which is his belonging to a truth-process. Or the manner in which our lover will be entirely 'himself' in the sustained testing of his inscription in a subject of love.

When all is said and done, consistency is the engagement of one's singularity (the animal 'some-one') in the continuation of a subject of truth. Or again: it is to submit the perseverance of what is known to a duration [*durée*] peculiar to the not-known.

Lacan touched on this point when he proposed his ethical maxim: 'do not give up on your desire' ['*ne pas céder sur son désir*']. For desire is constitutive of the subject of the unconscious; it is thus the not-known *par excellence*, such that 'do not give up on your desire' rightly means: 'do not give up on that part of yourself that you do not know'. We might add that the ordeal of the not-known is the distant effect of the evental supplement, the puncturing [*trouée*] of 'some-one' by a fidelity to this vanished supplement, and that 'do not give up' means, in the end: do not give up on your own seizure by a truth-process.

But since the truth-process is fidelity, then if 'Do not give up' is the maxim of consistency – and thus of the ethic of a truth – we might well say that it is a matter, for the 'some-one', of *being faithful to a fidelity*. And he can manage this only by adhering to his own principle of continuity, the perseverance in being of what he is. By *linking* (for such, precisely, is consistency) the known by the not-known.

It is now an easy matter to spell out the ethic of a truth: 'Do all that you can to persevere in that which exceeds your perseverance. Persevere in the interruption. Seize in your being that which has seized and broken you.'

The 'technique' of consistency is singular in each case, depending on the 'animal' traits of the some-one. To the consistency of the subject that he is in part become, having been convoked [*requis*] and seized by a truth-process, this particular 'some-one' will contribute his anguish and agitation, this other his tall stature and cool composure, this other his voracious taste for domination, and these others their melancholy, or timidity. . . . All the material of human multiplicity can be fashioned, linked, by a 'consistency' – while at the same time, of course, it opposes to this fashioning the worst kinds of inertia, and exposes the 'some-one' to the permanent temptation of giving up, of returning to the mere belonging to the 'ordinary' situation, of erasing the effects of the not-known.

The place of ethics is indicated by the chronic conflict between two functions of the multiple material that makes up the whole being of a 'some-one': on the one hand, its simple deployment, his belonging to the situation, or what we might call the *principle of interest*; on the other, consistency, the linking of the known by the not-known, or what we might call the *subjective principle*.

It is now a simple matter to describe the manifestations of consistency, to sketch a phenomenology of the ethic of truths.

III The experience of ethical 'consistency'

Consider two examples.

1. If we define interest as 'perseverance in being' (which is, remember, simply to belong to situations of multiplicity

[*aux situations multiples*]) then we can see that ethical consistency manifests itself as *disinterested interest*. It concerns interest, in the sense that it engages the motivating forces of perseverance (the singular traits of a human animal, of 'some-one'). But it is disinterested in a radical sense, since it aims to link these traits in a fidelity, which in its turn is addressed to a primary fidelity, the one that constitutes the truth-process and which, in itself, has nothing to do with the 'interests' of the animal, which is indifferent to its perpetuation, which has eternity for its destiny.

We might play here upon the ambiguity of the word *interest*. Certainly, the devotee of mathematics, the theatre spectator on the edge of his seat, the transfigured lover, the enthusiastic militant, demonstrate a prodigious interest in what they are doing – in the advent of the not-known Immortal in them, in the advent of that which they did not know themselves capable of. Nothing in the world could arouse the intensity of existence more than this actor who lets me encounter Hamlet, this perception in thought of what it means to be two, this problem in algebraic geometry whose innumerable ramifications I suddenly discover, or this open-air meeting, by the doors of a factory, which confirms that my political statement does indeed bring people together and transform them. Nevertheless, as regards my interests as a mortal and predatory animal, what is happening here does not concern me; no knowledge tells me that these circumstances have anything to do with me. I am altogether present there, linking my component elements via that *excess beyond myself* induced by the passing through me of a truth. But as a result, I am also suspended, broken, annulled; dis-interested. For I cannot, within the fidelity to fidelity that defines ethical consistency, take an interest in myself, and thus pursue my own interests. All my capacity for interest, which is my own perseverance in being, has *poured out* into the future consequences of the solution to this scientific problem, into the examination of the world in the light of love's being-two, into what I will make of my encounter, one night, with the eternal Hamlet, or into the next stage of the political process, once the gathering in front of the factory has dispersed.

There is always only one question in the ethic of truths: how will I, as some-one, *continue* to exceed my own being? How will I link the things I know, in a consistent fashion, via the effects of being seized by the not-known?

One might also put it like this: how will I continue *to think?* That is, to maintain *in* the singular time of my multiple-being, and with the sole material resources of this being, the Immortal that a truth brings into being through me in the composition of a subject.

2. Every truth, as we have seen, deposes constituted knowledges, and thus opposes opinions. For what we call *opinions* are representations without truth, the anarchic debris of circulating knowledge.

Now opinions are the cement of sociality [*socialité*]. They are what sustain all human animals, without exception, and we cannot function otherwise: the weather; the latest film; children's diseases; poor salaries; the government's villainy; the performance of the local football team; television; holidays; atrocities far away or close to home; the setbacks suffered by the Republican school system; the latest album by some hard-rock group; the delicate state of one's soul; whether or not there are too

many immigrants; neurotic symptoms; institutional success; good little recipes; what you've been reading; shops
in which you find what you need at a good price; cars;
sex; sunshine. . . . What would become of us, miserable
creatures, if all this did not circulate and recur among
the animals of the City? To what depressing silence
would we condemn ourselves? Opinion is the primary
material of all *communication*.

We are all familiar with the prestige enjoyed by this
term today, and we know that some see in it the foundation of democracy and ethics. Yes, it is often maintained
that what matters is to 'communicate', that all ethics is
'communicative ethics'.[2] If we ask: communicate, fine,
but communicate what?, then it is easy to answer: opinions, opinions regarding the whole expanse of multiples
that this special multiple, the human animal, explores in
the stubborn determination of his interests.

Opinions *without an ounce of truth* – or, indeed, of
falsehood. Opinion is beneath the true and the false,
precisely because its sole office is to be communicable.
What arises from a truth-process, by contrast, cannot be
communicated [*ne se communique pas*]. Communication
is suited only to opinions (and again, we are unable to
manage without them). In all that concerns truths, there
must be an *encounter*. The Immortal that I am capable of
being cannot be spurred in me by the effects of communicative sociality, it must be *directly* seized by fidelity. That
is to say: broken, in its multiple-being, by the course of
an immanent break, and convoked [*requis*], finally, with
or without knowing it, by the evental supplement. To
enter into the composition of a subject of truth can only
be something that *happens to you*.

Confirmation of the point is provided by the concrete circumstances in which someone is seized by a fidelity: an amorous encounter, the sudden feeling that this poem was addressed to you, a scientific theory whose initially obscure beauty overwhelms you, or the active intelligence of a political place. ... Philosophy is no exception here, since everyone knows that to endure the requirement of a philosophically disinterested-interest, you have to have encountered, at least once in your life, the voice of a Master.

As a result, the ethic of a truth is the complete opposite of an 'ethics of communication'. It is an ethic of the Real, if it is true that – as Lacan suggests – all access to the Real is of the order of an encounter. And consistency, which is the content of the ethical maxim 'Keep going!' [*Continuer!*], keeps going only by following the thread of this Real.

We might put it like this: 'Never forget what you have encountered.' But we can say this only if we understand that not-forgetting is not a memory (ah! the unbearable, journalistic 'ethics of memory'!). Not-forgetting consists of thinking and practising the arrangement of my multiple-being according to the Immortal which it holds, and which the piercing through [*transpercement*] of an encounter has composed as subject.

In one of my previous books, my formula was: 'Love what you will never believe twice' [*Aimez ce que jamais vous ne croirez deux fois*].[3] In this the ethic of a truth is absolutely opposed to opinion, and to ethics in general, which is itself nothing but a schema of opinion. For the maxim of opinion is: 'Love only that which you have always believed.'

IV Asceticism?

Is the ethic of truths ascetic? Does it always demand of us a renunciation? From the dawn of philosophy, this has been a crucial debate. It was already one of Plato's concerns, in his determination to prove that the philosopher, the man of truths, was 'happier' than the hedonistic tyrant, and that as a result, the sensual animal renounces nothing essential by dedicating its life to Ideas.

Let us call 'renunciation' the belief that we must cut back on the pursuit of our interests – the pursuit which, outside truth, constitutes the whole of our multiple-being. Is there renunciation when a truth seizes me? Certainly not, since this seizure manifests itself by unequalled intensities of existence. We can name them: in love, there is happiness; in science, there is joy (in Spinoza's sense: intellectual beatitude); in politics, there is enthusiasm; and in art, there is pleasure. These 'affects of truth', at the same moment that they signal the entry of some-one into a subjective composition, render empty all considerations of renunciation. Experience amply demonstrates the point, more than amply.

But ethics is not of the order of pure seizure. It regulates subjective consistency, inasmuch as its maxim is: 'Keep going!' And we have seen that this continuation presumes a genuine subversion [*détournement*] of the 'perseverance in being'. The materials of our multiple-being are now organized by the subjective composition, by fidelity to a fidelity, and no longer by the simple pursuit of our interest. Does this subversion amount to renunciation?

Here we have, it must be said, a properly *undecidable*

question. 'Undecidable' means that no calculation allows us to decide whether or not some essential renunciation is involved.

- On the one hand, it is certain that the ethic of truths compels so considerable a distance from opinions that it must be called literally *asocial*. This a-sociality has always been recognized for what it is – in the image of Thales falling into a well because he seeks to penetrate the secret of celestial movement;[4] in the proverb 'Lovers have eyes only for each other'; in the isolated destiny of the great revolutionary militants; in the theme of 'solitary genius', and so on. At the lowest level, you can see it in contemporary sarcasms about 'intellectuals', or the inevitable representation of the militant as 'dogmatic' or 'terrorist'. Now, a-sociality is constantly restricted in its pursuit of interests, because this pursuit is governed precisely by the social game, and by communication. It is not so much a question of repression here (although this obviously exists, and can take extreme forms) as of an insurmountable, properly ontological[5] clash between post-evental fidelity and the normal pace of things, between *truth* and *knowledge*.

- On the other hand, we must recognize that the 'myself' engaged in the subjective composition is identical to the one that pursues his interest: there cannot be, for us, two distinct figures of the 'some-one'. It is the same living multiples that are convoked [*requis*] in every case. This ambivalence of my multiple-composition ensures that interest can no longer be clearly represented as distinct from disinterested-interest. Every representation of myself is the fictional imposition of a unity upon infinite component multiples. There is no doubt that this fiction is generally held together by interest. But since the components are ambiguous (they are also the ones that serve to link my presence in a fidelity), it can happen that, under the same rule of interest, the fictional unity is organized as such around the subject, around the Immortal, and not around the socialized animal.

Basically, the *possibility* that no asceticism may be necessary for an ethic of truths testifies to the fact that the schema of interest has no other matter to unify, fictionally, than that to which the ethic of truths gives consistency. This means that disinterested-interest might be representable as interest pure and simple. Where this is the case, we cannot speak of asceticism: after all, the principle of interest governs [all] conscious practice.

But we are dealing here only with a simple possibility, and in no sense with a necessity. Let us not forget that *all* the components of my multiple-being could never be engaged together – no more, by the way, through the pursuit of my interests than through the consistency of a subject of truth. And so it can always happen that the brutal requisition of this or that 'dormant' component – under the socialized pressure of interests, or as an ongoing stage of a fidelity – might destabilize all the previous fictional assemblages through which I organized my self-representation. From this point, the perception of disinterested-interest as interest pure and simple may dissolve, the split may become representable, and asceticism may move on to the agenda – and, with it, its inversion: the temptation to give up, to withdraw from the subjective composition, to break a loving relationship because of the pull of an obscene desire, to betray a political sequence because of the repose promised by the 'service of goods' [*service des biens*],[6] to replace determined scientific investigation with the pursuit of recognition and awards, or to regress back to academicism under cover of a propaganda that denounces the avant-garde as '*passé*'.

But then the onset of asceticism is identical to the uncovering of the subject of truth as pure *desire of self* [*de soi*]. The subject must in some sense continue under his own steam, no longer protected by the ambiguities of the representing fiction. Such is the proper point of the undecidable: is this desire of the subject to persevere in his consistency congruent with the animal's desire to grab its socialized chance? Nothing, having come to this point, dispenses with the need for courage. Fortify yourself, if you can, with the optimism of Lacan, when he writes: 'Desire, what is called desire (Lacan is speaking here of the subjective not-known), suffices to prove that it would make no sense for life to create cowards.'[7]

Notes

1. Alain Badiou, *L'Etre et l'événement*, 1988. The theory of the event requires, in fact, certain lengthy conceptual detours, which are pursued in this book.
2. Jürgen Habermas, *The Theory of Communicative Action*, 2 vols, 1983–85. Habermas tries to extend 'democratic' rationality by integrating communication into the very foundations of his anthropology. From this point of view he contributes to what we might call the philosophical substructure of the 'ethical' current, from a position opposite to that of Lévinas.
3. Alain Badiou, *Théorie du sujet* [1982], 346. This book contains,

in its final chapters, some reflections on the ethics of the subject, though it is true that they are oriented in a slightly different way from those developed here.

4. [See Diogenes Laertius, *Lives of Eminent Philosophers*, i, 35. *Translator's note.*]

5. Badiou, *L'Etre et l'événement.* An element considered by opinion is always grasped in a *constructible* set (one that can be comprehended via classifications). Whereas the same element, considered from a truth-process, is caught up in a *generic* set (in brief: one that escapes all established classifications).

6. [*Le service des biens* is Lacan's phrase, referring to objects of 'normal' or consensual value, including 'private goods, family goods, domestic goods, other goods that solicit us, the goods of our trade or our profession, the goods of the city, etc.' (Jacques Lacan, *Séminaire VII*, 350/303; see also Badiou, *L'Etre et l'événement*, 375–6). *Translator's note.*]

7. Jacques Lacan, 'Kant avec Sade', in *Ecrits*, 782.

5

The Problem of Evil

I have already emphasized the degree to which our contemporary ethical ideology is rooted in the consensual self-evidence of Evil. We have overturned this judgement by determining the affirmative process of truths to be the central core both of the possible composition of a subject and – for the 'some-one' who enters into this composition – of the singular advent of a *persevering* ethic.

Is this to say that we must refuse the notion of Evil all validity, and refer it back exclusively to its obviously religious origin?

A Life, truths, and the Good

I will make no concessions here to those who believe that there is a kind of 'natural law', founded in the last analysis on the self-evidence of what is harmful to Man.

Considered in terms of its mere nature alone, the human animal must be lumped in the same category as its biological companions. This systematic killer pursues, in the giant ant hills he constructs, interests of survival and satisfaction neither more nor less estimable than those of moles or tiger beetles. He has shown himself to be the most wily of animals, the most patient, the most obstinately dedicated to the cruel desires of his own power. Above all, he has succeeded in harnessing to the service of his mortal life his own peculiar ability – his ability to take up a position along the course of truths such that he acquires an Immortal aspect. This is what Plato had already anticipated, when he indicated that the duty of those who escape from his famous cave, dazzled by the sun of the Idea, was to return to the shadows and to help their companions in servitude to profit from that by which, on the threshold of this dark world, they had been seized. Only today can we fully assess what this return means: it is that of Galilean physics back towards technical machinery, or of atomic theory back towards bombs and nuclear power plants. The return of disinterested-interest towards brute interest, the forcing of knowledges by a few truths. At the end of which the human animal has become the absolute master of his environment – which is, after all, nothing but a fairly mediocre planet.

Thus conceived (and this is what we know him to be), it is clear that the human animal, 'in itself', implies no value judgement. Nietzsche is no doubt right, once he has assessed humanity in terms of the norm of its vital power, to declare it essentially innocent, foreign in itself to both Good and Evil. His delusion is to imagine a superhumanity restored to this innocence, once delivered from the shadowy, life-destroying enterprise led by the powerful figure of the Priest.[1] No: no life, no natural power, can be beyond Good and Evil. We should say, rather, that every life, including that of the human animal, is *beneath* Good and Evil.

What provokes the emergence of the Good – and, by
simple consequence, Evil – exclusively concerns the rare
existence of truth-processes. Transfixed by an immanent
break, the human animal finds its principle of survival – its
interest – disorganized. We might say, then, if we accept
that some-one can enter into the composition of a subject
of truth, that the Good is, strictly speaking, the internal
norm of a prolonged disorganization of life.

In any case, everyone knows this: the routines of survival
are indifferent to any Good you might care to mention.
Every pursuit of an interest has success as its only source of
legitimacy. On the other hand, if I 'fall in love' (the word
'fall' indicates disorganization in the walk of life), or if I am
seized by the sleepless fury of a thought [*pensée*], or if some
radical political engagement proves incompatible with every
immediate principle of interest – then I find myself com-
pelled to measure life, my life as a socialized human animal,
against something other than itself. And this above all when,
beyond the joyful or enthusiastic clarity of the seizing, it
becomes a matter of finding out if, and how, I am to
continue along the path of vital disorganization, thereby
granting to this primordial disorganization a secondary and
paradoxical organization, that very organization which we
have called 'ethical consistency'.

If Evil exists, we must conceive it from the starting point
of the Good. Without consideration of the Good, and thus
of truths, there remains only the cruel innocence of life,
which is beneath Good *and beneath Evil.*

As a result – and however strange the suggestion may
seem – it is absolutely essential that Evil be a possible
dimension of truths. We cannot be satisfied, on this point,
with the overly facile Platonic solution: Evil as the simple

absence of truth, Evil as ignorance of the Good. For the very idea of ignorance is hard to grasp. For whom is a truth absent? For the human animal as such, absorbed in the pursuit of his interests, there is no truth, only opinions, through which he is socialized. As for the subject, the Immortal, he cannot lack the truth, since it is from the truth and the truth alone, given as faithful trajectory, that he constitutes himself.

If Evil is, all the same, identifiable as a form of multiple-being, it must then be that it arises as the (*possible*) *effect of the Good itself.* That is to say: it is only because there are truths, and only to the extent that there are subjects of these truths, that there is Evil.

Or again: Evil, if it exists, is an unruly effect of the power of truth.

But does Evil exist?

B   On the existence of Evil

Since we have entirely rejected the idea of a consensual or a priori recognition of Evil, the only rigorous line of thought open to us is to define Evil from within our own terrain, and thus as a possible dimension of a truth-process. Only then should we examine the overlap between the effects to be expected of this definition, and the 'flagrant' examples (the examples recognized by opinion) of historical or private Evil.

I shall nevertheless proceed in a more inductive fashion, since the aim of this book is to grasp the current dimension of these questions.

Those who uphold 'ethical' ideology know very well that

the identification of Evil is no trifling matter, even if, in the
end, their whole construction rests on the axiom that the
issue remains a self-evident matter of opinion. Their strategy
is then the same as that of Lévinas with respect to the
'recognition of the other': they radicalize their thesis. Just
as Lévinas eventually makes the originality of the opening
to the Other depend upon the supposition of the
Altogether-Other, so the upholders of ethics make the
consensual identification of Evil depend upon the supposition of a *radical* Evil.

Although the idea of a radical Evil can be traced back at
least as far as Kant, its contemporary version is grounded
systematically on one 'example': the Nazi extermination of
the European Jews. I do not use the word 'example' lightly.
An ordinary example is indeed something to be repeated
or imitated. Relating to the Nazi extermination, it exempli-
fies radical Evil by pointing to that whose imitation or
repetition must be prevented at all costs – or, more precisely: that whose non-repetition provides the norm for the
judgement of all situations. Hence the 'exemplarity' of the
crime, its negative exemplarity. But the normative function
of the example persists: the Nazi extermination is radical
Evil in that it provides for our time the unique, unrivalled –
and in this sense transcendent, or unsayable – measure of
Evil pure and simple. What the God of Lévinas is to the
evaluation of alterity (the Altogether-Other as incommensurable measure of the Other), the extermination is to the
evaluation of historical situations (the Altogether-Evil as
incommensurable measure of Evil).

As a result, the extermination and the Nazis are both
declared unthinkable, unsayable, without conceivable prec-
edent or posterity – since they define the absolute form of

Evil – yet they are constantly invoked, compared, used to schematize every circumstance in which one wants to produce, among opinions, an effect of the awareness [*conscience*] of Evil – since the only way to access Evil in general is under the historical condition of radical Evil. So it was as early as 1956, in order to justify the Anglo-French invasion of Egypt, some Western political leaders and the press did not hesitate for a second to use the formula 'Nasser is Hitler'. We have seen the same thing again more recently, as much with Saddam Hussein (in Iraq) as with Slobodan Milošević (in Serbia). But at the same time, we are insistently reminded that the extermination and the Nazis were unique, and that to compare them to anything else at all is a defilement.

In fact, this paradox is simply that of radical Evil itself (and, in truth, of every '*mise en transcendence*' of a reality or concept). The measure must itself be unmeasurable, yet it must constantly be measured. The extermination is indeed both that which measures all the Evil our time is capable of, being itself beyond measure, and that to which we must compare everything (thus measuring it unceasingly) that we say is to be judged in terms of the manifest certainty of Evil. As the supreme negative example, this crime is inimitable, but every crime is an imitation of it.

To get out of this circle, to which we are condemned by the fact that we want to subordinate the question of Evil to a consensual judgement of opinion (a judgement that then has to be pre-structured by the supposition of a radical Evil), we obviously have to abandon the theme of radical Evil, of the measure without measure. This theme, like that of the Altogether-Other, belongs to religion.

It goes without saying, of course, that the extermination

of the European Jews is a hideous state crime, whose horror
is such that whichever way we look at it, we know – unless
we are prepared to stoop to repulsive sophistry – that we
are confronted by an Evil that cannot in any sense be
quietly ('Hegelian-ly') classified among the transitory necessities of the Historical process.

I further accept, without reservation, the singularity of
the extermination. The bland category of 'totalitarianism'
was forged in order to group under a single concept the
politics of Nazism and of Stalinism, the extermination of
the European Jews and the massacres in Siberia. This amal-
gamation does nothing to clarify our thinking, not even our
thinking about Evil. We must accept the irreducibility of the
extermination (just as we must accept the irreducibility of
the Stalinist Party-state).

But then the whole point is to situate [localiser] this
singularity. Fundamentally, those who uphold the ideology
of human rights try to situate it directly in Evil, in keeping
with their objectives of pure opinion. We have seen that this
attempt at the religious absolutization of Evil is incoherent.
Moreover, it is very threatening, like anything that puts
thought up against an impassable 'limit'. For the reality of
the inimitable is constant imitation, and by dint of seeing
Hitlers everywhere we forget that he is dead, and that what
is happening before our eyes is the creation of new singularities of Evil.

In fact, to think the singularity of the extermination is to
think, first of all, the singularity of Nazism as a political
sequence. This is the whole problem. Hitler was able to
conduct the extermination as a colossal militarized operation because he had taken power, and he took power in the
name of a politics whose categories included the term 'Jew'.

The defenders of ethical ideology are so determined to locate the singularity of the extermination directly in Evil that they generally deny, categorically, that Nazism was a political sequence. But this position is both feeble and cowardly. Feeble, because the constitution of Nazism as a 'massive' subjectivity integrating the word Jew as part of a political configuration is what made the extermination possible, and then inevitable. Cowardly, because it is impossible to think politics through to the end if we refuse to envisage the possibility of political sequences whose organic categories and subjective prescriptions are criminal. The partisans of the 'democracy of human rights' are fond – with Hannah Arendt – of defining politics as the stage of a 'being-together'. It is with regard to this definition, incidentally, that they fail to grasp the political essence of Nazism. But this definition is merely a fairy-tale – all the more so since the being-together must first determine the collective [*ensemble*] concerned, and this is the whole question. Nobody desired the being-together of the Germans more than Hitler. The Nazi category of the 'Jew' served to name the German interior, the space of a being-together, via the (arbitrary yet prescriptive) construction of an exterior that could be monitored from the interior – just as the certainty of being 'all French together' presupposes that we persecute, here and now, those who fall under the category of 'illegal immigrant'.

One of the singularities of Nazi politics was its precise proclamation of the historical community that was to be endowed with a conquering *subjectivity*. And it was this proclamation that enabled its subjective victory, and put extermination on the agenda.

Thus we are entitled to say, in this case, that the link

between politics and Evil emerges precisely from the way both the collective [*ensemble*] (the thematics of communities) and the being-with (the thematics of consensus, of shared norms) are taken into consideration.

But what matters is that the singularity of the Evil derives, in the final analysis, from the singularity of a political sequence.

This takes us back to the subordination of Evil – if not directly to the Good, at least to the processes that lay claim to it. Nazi politics was not a truth-process, but it was only in so far as it could be represented as such that it 'seized' the German situation. So that even in the case of this Evil, which I would call extreme rather than radical, the intelligibility of its 'subjective' being, the question of the 'some-ones' who were able to participate in its horrifying execution as if accomplishing a duty, needs to be referred back to the intrinsic dimensions of the process of political truth.

I might also have pointed out that the most intense subjective sufferings – those that really highlight what is involved in 'hurting someone', and often lead to suicide or murder – have as their horizon the existence of a process of love.

I shall posit the following general principles:

- that Evil exists;
- that it must be distinguished from the violence that the human animal employs to persevere in its being, to pursue its interests – a violence that is *beneath* Good and Evil;
- that nevertheless there is no radical Evil, which might otherwise clarify this distinction;

- that Evil can be considered as distinct from banal preda-
  tion only in so far as we grasp it from the perspective of
  the Good, thus from the seizing of 'some-one' by a truth-
  process;
- that as a result, Evil is a category not of the human
  animal, but of the subject;
- that there is Evil only to the extent that man is capable of
  becoming the Immortal he is;
- that the ethic of truths – as the principle of consistency
  of a fidelity to a fidelity, or the maxim 'Keep going!' – is
  what tries to ward off the Evil that every singular truth
  makes possible.

We still have to link these propositions together, to make
them consistent with what we know about the general form
of truths.

C   Return to the event, fidelity and truth

Remember that the three major dimensions of a truth-
process are as follows:

- the *event*, which brings to pass 'something other' than the
  situation, opinions, instituted knowledges; the event is a
  hazardous [*hasardeux*], unpredictable supplement, which
  vanishes as soon as it appears;
- the *fidelity*, which is the name of the process: it amounts
  to a sustained investigation of the situation, under the
  imperative of the event itself; it is an immanent and
  continuing break;
- the *truth* as such, that is, the multiple, internal to the

situation, that the fidelity constructs, bit by bit; it is what the fidelity gathers together and produces.

These three dimensions of the process have several essential 'ontological' characteristics.

1. The event is both *situated* – it is the event of this or that situation – and *supplementary*; thus absolutely detached from, or unrelated to, all the rules of the situation. Hence the emergence of the classical style, with Haydn (or under the name of this 'some-one', Haydn), concerns the musical situation and no other, a situation then governed by the predominance of the baroque style. It was an event for this situation. But in another sense, what this event was to authorize in terms of musical configurations was not comprehensible from within the plenitude achieved by the baroque style; it really was a matter of *something else*.

   You might then ask what it is that makes the connection between the event and that 'for which' it is an event. This connection is the void [*vide*] of the earlier situation. What does this mean? It means that at the heart of every situation, as the foundation of its being, there is a 'situated' void, around which is organized the plenitude (or the stable multiples) of the situation in question. Thus at the heart of the baroque style at its virtuoso saturation lay the absence [*vide*] (as decisive as it was unnoticed) of a genuine conception of musical architectonics. The Haydn-event occurs as a kind of musical 'naming' of this absence [*vide*]. For what constitutes the event is nothing less than a wholly new architectonic and thematic principle, a new way of developing musical

writing from the basis of a few transformable units –
which was precisely what, from within the baroque style,
could not be perceived (there could be no knowledge of
it).

We might say that since a situation is composed by the
knowledges circulating within it, the event names the void
inasmuch as it names the not-known of the situation.

To take a well-known example: Marx is an event for
political thought because he designates, under the name
'proletariat', the central void of early bourgeois societies.
For the proletariat – being entirely dispossessed, and
absent from the political stage – is that around which is
organized the complacent plenitude established by the
rule of those who possess capital.

To sum up: the fundamental ontological characteristic
of an event is to inscribe, to name, the situated void of
that for which it is an event.

2. As for fidelity, I have already explained what is at stake.
The essential point is that it is never inevitable or necessary.
What remains undecidable is whether the disinterested-
interest that it presumes on the part of the 'some-one'
who participates in it can, even if only as part of a
fictional representation of self, count as interest pure
and simple. And so, since the sole principle of perseverance is that of interest, the perseverance of some-one in
a fidelity – the continuation of the being-subject of a
human animal – remains uncertain. We know that it is
because of this uncertainty that there is a place for an
ethic of truths.

3. Finally, as regards the truth that results, we must above
all emphasize its power. I have already evoked this

theme, with respect to the 'return' to the cave of Plato's prisoner, which is the return of a truth back to knowledges. A truth punches a 'hole' in knowledges, it is heterogeneous to them, but it is also the sole known source of new knowledges. We shall say that the truth *forces* knowledges.[2] The verb *to force* indicates that since the power of a truth is that of a break, it is by violating established and circulating knowledges that a truth returns to the immediacy [*l'immédiat*] of the situation, or reworks that sort of portable encyclopaedia from which opinions, communications and sociality draw their meaning. If a truth is never communicable as such, it nevertheless implies, at a distance from itself, powerful reshapings of the forms and referents of communication. This is not to say that these modifications 'express' the truth, or indicate 'progress' among opinions. For instance, a whole body of musical knowledge was quickly organized around the great names of the classical style – a knowledge that could not previously have been formulated. There is no 'progress' here, for classical academicism, or the cult of Mozart, are in no sense superior to what went on before. But it marks a forcing of knowledges, an often extensive modification of the codes of communication (or the opinions on 'music' that human animals swap). Of course, these modified opinions are ephemeral, whereas the truths themselves, which are the great creations of the classical style, shall endure eternally.

In the same way, it is the eventual destiny of the most astonishing mathematical inventions to wind up in college textbooks, even to help decide the selection of our 'governing elite' via the entrance exams to the *Grandes Ecoles*.[3] The eternity produced from mathematical truths is not itself at issue here, but they have *forced* knowledges required in this fashion for the arranging of sociality, and such is the form of their return back to the interests of the human animal.

It is upon these three dimensions of the process of truth – the convocation by an event of the *void* of a situation; the uncertainty of *fidelity*; and the powerful *forcing* of knowledges by a truth – that the thought of Evil depends.

For Evil has three names:

• to believe that an event convokes not the void of the earlier situation, but its plenitude, is Evil in the sense of *simulacrum*, or *terror*;
• to fail to live up to a fidelity is Evil in the sense of *betrayal*, betrayal in oneself of the Immortal that you are;
• to identify a truth with total power is Evil in the sense of *disaster*.

Terror, betrayal and disaster are what an ethic of truths – as opposed to the impotent morality of human rights – tries to ward off, in the singularity of its reliance on a truth in progress. But as we shall see, these have become real possibilities only through the truth-process itself. And so it is certain that there can be Evil only in so far as there proceeds a Good [*qu'autant que procède un Bien*].

D   Outline of a theory of Evil

I   Simulacrum and terror

We have seen that not every 'novelty' is an event. It must further be the case that what the event calls forth and names is the central void of the situation for which this event is an event. This matter of nomination is essential, and I cannot go through the complete theory of it here.[4] But it should be easy to understand that since the event *is* to disappear, being a kind of flashing supplement that happens to the situation, so what is retained of it in the situation, and what serves to guide the fidelity, must be something like a trace, or a name, that refers back to the vanished event.

When the Nazis talked about the 'National Socialist revolution', they borrowed names – 'revolution', 'socialism' – justified by great modern political events (the Revolution of 1792, or the Bolshevik Revolution of 1917). A whole series of characteristics are related to and legitimated by this borrowing: the break with the old order, the support sought from mass gatherings, the dictatorial style of the state, the *pathos* of the decision, the eulogy of the Worker, and so forth.

However, the 'event' thus named – although in certain formal respects it is similar to those from which it borrows its name and characteristics, and without which it would have no constituted political language in which to formulate proposals of its own – is distinguished by a vocabulary of plenitude, or of substance: the National Socialist revolution – say the Nazis – will carry a particular community, the

German people, towards its true destiny, which is a destiny of universal domination. So that the 'event' is supposed to bring into being, and name, not the void of the earlier situation, but its plenitude – not the universality of that which is sustained, precisely, by no particular characteristic (no particular multiple), but the absolute particularity of a community, itself rooted in the characteristics of its soil, its blood, and its race.

What allows a genuine event to be at the origin of a truth – which is the only thing that can be for all, and can be eternally – is precisely the fact that it relates to the particularity of a situation only from the bias of its void. The void, the multiple-of-nothing, neither excludes nor constrains anyone. It is the absolute neutrality of being – such that the fidelity that originates in an event, although it is an immanent break within a singular situation, is none the less universally addressed.

By contrast, the striking break provoked by the Nazi seizure of power in 1933, although formally indistinguishable from an event – it is precisely this that led Heidegger astray[5] – since it conceives itself as a 'German' revolution, and is faithful only to the alleged national substance of a people, is actually addressed only to those that it itself deems 'German'. It is thus – right from the moment the event is named, and despite the fact that this nomination ('revolution') functions only under the condition of true universal events (for example the Revolutions of 1792 or 1917) – radically incapable of any truth whatsoever.

When a radical break in a situation, under names borrowed from real truth-processes, convokes not the void but the 'full' particularity or presumed substance of that situation, we are dealing with a *simulacrum of truth*.

'Simulacrum' must be understood here in its strong sense: all the formal traits of a truth are at work in the simulacrum. Not only a universal nomination of the event, inducing the power of a radical break, but also the 'obligation' of a fidelity, and the promotion of a *simulacrum of the subject*, erected – without the advent of any Immortal – above the human animality of the others, of those who are arbitrarily declared not to belong to the communitarian substance whose promotion and domination the simulacrum-event is designed to assure.

Fidelity to a simulacrum, unlike fidelity to an event, regulates its break with the situation not by the universality of the void, but by the closed particularity of an abstract set [*ensemble*] (the 'Germans' or the 'Aryans'). Its invariable operation is the unending construction of this set, and it has no other means of doing this than that of 'voiding' what surrounds it. The void, 'avoided' [*chassé*] by the simulacrous promotion of an 'event-substance', here returns, with its universality, as what must be accomplished in order that this substance can be. This is to say that what is addressed 'to everyone' (and 'everyone', here, is necessarily that which does not belong to the German communitarian substance – for this substance is not an 'everyone' but, rather, some 'few' who dominate 'everyone') is death, or that deferred form of death which is slavery in the service of the German substance.

Hence fidelity to the simulacrum (and it demands of the 'few' belonging to the German substance prolonged sacrifices and commitments, since it really does have the form of a fidelity) has as its content war and massacre. These are not here means to an end: they make up the very real [*tout le réel*][6] of such a fidelity.

In the case of Nazism, the void made its return under one privileged name in particular, the name 'Jew'. There were certainly others as well: the Gypsies, the mentally ill, homosexuals, communists. . . . But the name 'Jew' was the name of names, serving to designate those people whose disappearance created, around that presumed German substance promoted by the 'National Socialist revolution' simulacrum, a void that would suffice to identify the substance. The choice of this name relates, without any doubt, to its obvious link with universalism, in particular with revolutionary universalism – to what was in effect already *void* [*vide*] about this name – that is, what was *connected to the universality and eternity of truths.* Nevertheless, inasmuch as it served to organize the extermination, the name 'Jew' was a political creation of the Nazis, without any pre-existing referent. It is a name whose meaning no one can share with the Nazis, a meaning that presumes the simulacrum and fidelity to the simulacrum – and hence the absolute singularity of Nazism as a political sequence.

But even in this respect, we have to recognize that this process mimics an actual truth-process. Every fidelity to an authentic event names the adversaries of its perseverance. Contrary to consensual ethics, which tries to avoid divisions, the ethic of truths is always more or less militant, combative. For the concrete manifestation of its heterogeneity to opinions and established knowledges is the struggle against all sorts of efforts at interruption, at corruption, at the return to the immediate interests of the human animal, at the humiliation and repression of the Immortal who arises as subject. The ethic of truths presumes recognition of these efforts, and thus the singular operation of naming enemies. The 'National Socialist revolution' simulacrum encouraged

nominations of this kind, in particular the nomination of
'Jew'. But the simulacrum's subversion of the true event
continues with these namings. For the enemy of a true
subjective fidelity is precisely the closed set [*ensemble*], the
substance of the situation, the community. The values of
truth, of its hazardous course and its universal address, are
to be erected against these forms of inertia.

Every invocation of blood and soil, of race, of custom, of
community, works directly against truths; and it is this very
collection [*ensemble*] that is named as the enemy in the ethic
of truths. Whereas fidelity to the simulacrum, which promotes the community, blood, race, and so on, names as its
enemy – for example, under the name of 'Jew' – precisely
the abstract universality and eternity of truths, the address
to all.

Moreover, the two processes treat what is thus named in
diametrically opposite ways. For however hostile to a truth
he might be, in the ethic of truths every 'some-one' is always
represented as capable of becoming the Immortal that he
is. So we may fight against the judgements and opinions he
exchanges with others for the purpose of corrupting every
fidelity, but not against his *person* – which, under the
circumstances, is insignificant, and to which, in any case,
every truth is ultimately addressed. By contrast, the void
with which those who are faithful to a simulacrum strive to
surround its alleged substance must be a real void, obtained
by cutting into the flesh itself. And since it is not the
subjective advent of an Immortal, so fidelity to the simulacrum – that appalling imitation of truths – presumes
nothing more about those they designate as the enemy than
their strictly particular existence as human animals. It is
thus this existence that will have to bear the return of the

void. This is why the exercise of fidelity to the simulacrum is necessarily the exercise of terror. Understand by terror, here, not the political concept of Terror, linked (in a universalizable couple) to the concept of Virtue by the Immortals of the Jacobin Committee of Public Safety, but the pure and simple reduction of all to their being-for-death. Terror thus conceived really postulates that in order to let [the] substance be, *nothing* must be [*pour que la substance soit,* rien *ne doit être*].

I have pursued the example of Nazism because it enters to a significant extent into that 'ethical' configuration (of 'radical Evil') opposed by the ethic of truths. What is at issue here is the simulacrum of an event that gives rise to a political fidelity. Such a simulacrum is possible only thanks to the success of political revolutions that were genuinely evental (and thus universally addressed). But simulacra linked to all the other possible kinds of truth-processes also exist. The reader may find it useful to identify them. For example, we can see how certain sexual passions are simulacra of the amorous event. There can be no doubt that on this account they bring with them terror and violence. Likewise, brutal obscurantist preachings present themselves as the simulacra of science, with obviously damaging results. And so on. But in each case, these violent damages are unintelligible if we do not understand them in relation to the truth-processes whose simulacra they manipulate.

In sum, our first definition of Evil is this: Evil is the process of a simulacrum of truth. And in its essence, under a name of its invention, it is terror directed at everyone.

II Betrayal

I began the explanation of this point in Chapter 4. We
have seen that it cannot be decided for sure whether the
disinterested-interest that animates the becoming-subject of
a human animal prevails over interest pure and simple,
once this human animal can no longer manage to unify the
two kinds of interest in a plausible fiction of his own unity.

We are dealing here with what might be called moments
of crisis. 'It itself', a truth-process is untouched by crisis.
Initiated by an event, in principle it extends to infinity.
What can go into crisis is the one or several 'some-ones'
who enter into the composition of the subject induced by
this process. Everyone is familiar with the moments of crisis
faced by a lover, a researcher's discouragement, a militant's
lassitude, an artist's sterility. Or again, with the lasting
failure of someone to understand a mathematical proof,
with the irreducible obscurity of a poem whose beauty one
can nevertheless dimly perceive, and so forth.

I have explained where such experiences come from:
under pressure from the demands of interest – or, on the
contrary, because of difficult new demands within the subjective continuation of fidelity – there is a breakdown of the
fiction I use to maintain, as an image of myself, the confusion between my ordinary interests and disinterested-
interest, between human animal and subject, between
mortal and immortal. And at this point, I am confronted
with a pure choice between the 'Keep going!' proposed by
the ethic of this truth, and the logic of the 'perseverance in
being' of the mere mortal that I am.

A crisis of fidelity is always what puts to the test, following the collapse of an image, the sole maxim of consistency (and thus of ethics): 'Keep going!' Keep going even when you have lost the thread, when you no longer feel 'caught up' in the process, when the event itself has become obscure, when its name is lost, or when it seems that it may have named a mistake, if not a simulacrum.

For the well-known existence of simulacra is a powerful stimulus to the crystallization of crises. Opinion tells me (and therefore I tell myself, for I am never outside opinions) that my fidelity may well be terror exerted against myself, and that the fidelity to which I am faithful looks very much like – too much like – this or that certified Evil. It is always a possibility, since the formal characteristics of this Evil (as simulacrum) are exactly those of a truth.

What I am then exposed to is the temptation to *betray* a truth. Betrayal is not mere renunciation. Unfortunately, one cannot simply 'renounce' a truth. The denial of the Immortal in myself is something quite different from an abandonment, a cessation: I must always convince myself that the Immortal in question *never existed*, and thus rally to opinion's perception of this point – opinion, whose whole purpose, in the service of interests, is precisely this negation. For the Immortal, if I recognize its existence, calls on me to continue; it has the eternal power of the truths that induce it. Consequently, I must betray the becoming-subject in myself, I must become the enemy of that truth whose subject the 'some-one' that I am (accompanied, perhaps, by others) composed.

This explains why former revolutionaries are obliged to declare that they used to be lost in error and madness, why a former lover no longer understands why he loved that woman, why a tired scientist comes to misunderstand, and to frustrate through bureaucratic routine, the very development of his own science. Since the process of truth is an immanent break, you can 'leave' it (which is to say, according to Lacan's powerful phrase, return to the 'service of goods' [*service des biens*]) only by breaking with this break which has seized you. And this breaking of a break has continuity as its motif [*motif*]. Continuity of the situation and continuity of opinions: all that came before, under the names of 'politics' or 'love', was an illusion at best, a simulacrum at worst.

So it is that the defeat of the ethic of a truth, at the undecidable point of a crisis, presents itself as betrayal.

And this is an Evil from which there is no return; betrayal is the second name, after simulacrum, of the Evil made possible by a truth.

III The unnameable

I have said that a truth transforms the codes of communication and changes the regime of opinions – such is its effect of 'return'. Not that these opinions become 'true' (or false). They are not capable of truth, and a truth, in its eternal multiple-being, remains indifferent to opinions. But they become *other*. This means that formerly obvious judgements are no longer defensible, that others become necessary, that the means of communication change, and so on.

I have called this reorganization of opinions the *power* [*puissance*] of truths.

The question we must now ask ourselves is this: does the power of a truth, in the situation in which it pursues its faithful course, have the potential to be total?

What exactly is implied by the hypothesis of a truth's *total* power? To understand this, we have to remember our onto-logical axioms: an (objective) situation, in particular one in which a (subjective) truth is 'at work', is never anything other than a multiple, made up of an infinity of elements (which are themselves multiples in their turn). What, then, is the general form of an opinion? An opinion is a judgement applied to this or that element of the objective situation – 'It's stormy today'; 'I tell you: all politicians are corrupt', and so on. In order to be able to 'discuss' the elements of a situation – which are all that belong to this situation – they have to be named in one way or another. 'To name' simply implies that human animals are in a position to communi-cate about these elements, to socialize their existence and arrange them in terms of their interests.

Let us call 'language of the situation' the pragmatic possibility of naming the elements that compose it, and thus of exchanging opinions about them.

Every truth is likewise concerned with the elements of the situation, since its process is nothing other than their examination *from the perspective of the event*. In this sense, the truth-process identifies these elements, and some-one who enters into the composition of a subject of truth will cer-tainly contribute to this identification by using the language of the situation, which, as a 'some-one', he uses just like everyone else. From this point of view, the truth-process passes through the language of the situation, just as it passes through its every knowledge.

But the examination of an element according to a truth is something entirely different from its pragmatic evaluation [*jugement*] in terms of opinion. It is not a matter of accom-modating this element to the interests of human animals, which are in any case divergent since opinions contradict each other. It simply amounts to evaluating this element 'in truth' with respect to the immanent, post-evental break. This evaluation is itself disinterested; it seeks to endow the element with a kind of eternity, in keeping with the becoming-Immortal of the 'some-ones' who participate in the subject of truth, the subject which provides the real basis of the evaluation.

From this follows a crucial result: in the end, a truth *changes the names* of elements in the situation. This means that its own naming of the elements is something other than pragmatic nomination, as much in its point of departure (the event, the fidelity) as in its destination (an eternal truth). And this is the case even if the truth-process passes through the language of the situation.

We must admit, then, that in addition to the language of the objective situation, which enables the communication of opinions, there exists a subject-language [*langue-sujet*] (the language of the subjective situation) which enables the inscription of a truth.

In fact, this is a self-evident point. The mathematized language of science is in no way the language of opinions, including opinions on science. The language of a declaration of love may be very banal indeed ('I love you', for example), but its *power* in the situation is nevertheless entirely distinct from the common usage of these same words. The language of a poem is not that of a journalist. And the language of politics is so peculiar that to the ears of opinion it sounds like jargon ['*langue de bois*'].

The important thing is that the power of a truth, directed at opinions, forces the pragmatic namings (the language of the objective situation) to bend and change shape upon contact with the subject-language. It is this and only this that changes the established codes of communication, under the impact of a truth.

We can now define what the *total* power of a truth would be: it would imply the ability to name and evaluate *all* the elements of the objective situation from the perspective of the truth-process. Rigid and dogmatic (or 'blinded'), the subject-language would claim the power, based on its own axioms, to name the whole of the real, and thus to change the world.

The powers of the language of the situation are themselves, to be sure, unrestricted: every element can be named from the perspective of a given interest, and judged in the communication between human animals. But since this language is in any case incoherent, and dedicated to pragmatic exchange, its totalizing vocation does not matter much.

By contrast, when we come to the subject-language (the language of the militant, the researcher, the artist, the lover . . .), which is the result of a truth-process, the hypothesis of total power here has consequences of an altogether different order.

In the first place, we thereby presume that the totality of the objective situation can be organized in terms of the particular *coherence* of a subjective truth.

We next assume that it is possible to eliminate opinion. For if the subject-language covers the same ground as the language of the situation, if truth can be pronounced with respect to every element, then the power of a truth would manifest itself not by the mere distortion of pragmatic and communicative meanings, but by the absolute authority of truthful nomination. A truth would then force the pure and simple replacement of the language of the situation by a subject-language. That is to say: the Immortal would come into being as the wholesale negation of the human animal that bears him.

When Nietzsche proposes to 'break the history of the world in two' by exploding Christian nihilism and generalizing the great Dionysian 'yes' to Life; or when certain Red Guards of the Chinese Cultural Revolution proclaim, in 1967, the complete suppression of self-interest, they are indeed inspired by a vision of a situation in which all interest has disappeared, and in which opinions have been *replaced* by the truth to which Nietzsche and the Red Guards are committed. The great nineteenth-century positivists likewise imagined that the statements of science were going to *replace* opinions and beliefs about all things. And the German Romantics worshipped a universe entirely transfixed by an absolutized poetics.

But Nietzsche went mad. The Red Guards, after inflicting immense harm, were imprisoned or shot, or betrayed by their own fidelity. Our century has been the graveyard of positivist ideas of progress. And the Romantics, already prone to suicide, were to see their 'literary absolute' engender monsters in the form of 'aestheticized politics'.[7]

For every truth presumes, in fact, in the composition of the subjects it induces, the preservation of 'some-one', the always two-sided activity of the human animal caught up in truth. Even ethical 'consistency', as we have seen, is only the disinterested engagement, in fidelity, of a perseverance whose origin is interest – such that every attempt to impose the total power of a truth ruins that truth's very foundation [*support*].

The Immortal exists only in and by the mortal animal. Truths make their singular penetration [*percée*] only through the fabric of opinions. We all need to communicate, we must all express our opinions. It is we ourselves, as ourselves, who expose ourselves to the becoming-subject. There is no History other than our own; there is no true world to come. The world as world is, and will remain beneath the true and the false. There is no world that might be captive to the coherence of the Good. The world is, and will remain, beneath Good and Evil.

The Good is Good only to the extent that it does not aspire to render the world good. Its sole being lies in the situated advent [*l'advenue en situation*] of a singular truth. So it must be that the power of a truth is also a kind of powerlessness.

Every absolutization of the power of a truth organizes an Evil. Not only does this Evil destroy the situation (for the will to eliminate opinion is, fundamentally, the same as the will to eliminate, in the human animal, its very animality, i.e. its being), but it also interrupts the truth-process in whose name it proceeds, since it fails to preserve, within the composition of its subject, the duality [*duplicité*] of interests (disinterested-interest and interest pure and simple).

This is why I will call this figure of Evil a disaster, a disaster of the truth induced by the absolutization of its power.

That truth does not have total power means, in the last analysis, that the subject-language, the production of a truth-process, does not have the power to name all the elements of the situation. At least one real element must exist, one multiple existing in the situation, which remains inaccessible to truthful nominations, and is exclusively reserved to opinion, to the language of the situation. At least one point that the truth cannot force.

I shall call this element the unnameable of a truth.[8]

The unnameable is not so 'in itself': it is potentially accessible to the language of the situation, and we can certainly exchange opinions about it. For there is no limit to communication. The unnameable is unnameable *for* the subject-language. Let us say that this term is not susceptible of being made eternal, or not accessible to the Immortal. In this sense, it is the symbol of the pure real [*réel*] of the situation, of its life without truth.

To determine the unnameable point of a particular type of truth-process is a difficult task for (philosophical) thought. There can be no question of undertaking this determination here. So I shall simply say that as far as love is concerned, it can be established that sexual pleasure [*jouissance*] as such is inaccessible to the power of the truth (which is a truth about the *two*). For mathematics, which represents non-contradictory thought *par excellence*, it is precisely non-contradiction that cannot be named: we know that it is indeed impossible to prove, from within a mathematical system, the non-contradiction of that system (this is Gödel's famous theorem).[9] Finally, the community and the collective are the unnameables of political truth: every attempt 'politically' to name a community induces a disastrous Evil (which can be seen as much in the extreme example of Nazism as in the reactionary usage of the word 'French', whose entire purpose is to persecute some of those who live here in France under the arbitrary imputation of being 'foreigners').

What matters here is the general principle: Evil in this case is to want, at all costs and under condition of a truth, to force the naming of the unnameable. Such, exactly, is the principle of disaster.

Simulacrum (associated with the event), betrayal (associated with the fidelity), and the forcing of the unnameable (associated with the power of the true): these are the figures of Evil, an Evil which becomes an *actual* possibility only thanks to the sole Good we recognize – a truth-process.

Notes

1. Friedrich Nietzsche, *The Genealogy of Morals*. This is Nietzsche's most systematic book, the one that sums up his 'vital' critique of values.

2. [*Forcing* is what happens 'between' truth and knowledge; although only a truth 'forces', 'forcing is a relation that is verifiable by knowledge' (*L'Etre et l'événement*, 441). In the considerably more technical pages of *L'Etre et l'événement*, Badiou explains that 'forcing' is the process, imposed by the affirmation of a truth, whereby the order of knowledge in a situation is transformed such that this previously 'unrecognizable' affirmation can be made to *belong* to the situation. For if it persists, 'a truth will force the situation to arrange itself in such a way that this truth, to begin with counted only as an anonymous part [or subset of a set], will finally be recognized as a term [or element of a set], and as internal to the situation' (ibid., 377). More precisely: that a term of the situation (i.e. an event) 'forces a statement of the subject-language means that the verifiability of this statement in the situation to come is equivalent to the belonging of this term to the indiscernible part [or subset] that results from the generic procedure' (ibid., 441: what remains forever unverifiable by knowledge, of course, is whether the event itself – that is, the term that forced the statement – belongs or does not belong to the situation). The positive 'connection' of this statement will be verifiable, know-able, in the transformed, post-evental situation.

In its more strictly mathematical sense, first proposed by Paul Cohen in the early 1960s (in a study which in some ways figures as *the* event 'behind' *L'Etre et l'événement* itself), 'forcing' is the process by which a generic subset or 'extension' is added to a set and then made to *belong* to that set. 'The crucial idea [involved in "forcing"] will be the preferential treatment of the universal quantifier [∀: "for all . . ."] over the existential quantifier [∃: "there exists"]' (Paul Cohen, *Set Theory and the Continuum Hypothesis*, 112). Forcing privileges, in other words, a minimally specified universality over any established or definitive particularity. The mathematical demonstration of this process is too complicated even to summarize here (see, for instance, John P. Burgess, 'Forcing', in Barwise, ed., *Handbook of Mathematical Logic*, 403–53). *Translator's note.*]

3. [The various *Grandes Ecoles* – L'Ecole Normale Supérieure, L'Ecole Polytechnique, L'Ecole Nationale de l'Administration, etc. – were set up by Napoleon to co-ordinate the recruitment of an elite civil service, and continue to retain an immense cultural and academic prestige in France today. Since 1999, Badiou himself has taught philosophy at the Ecole Normale Supérieure, in the position previously occupied by his own teacher, Louis Althusser. *Translator's note.*]

4. See Badiou, *L'Etre et l'événement*, meditations 20, 34. The theory of the name of the event, on the one hand, and of the subject-language on the other, is central to the whole book. The second question, in particular, is fairly tricky.

5. Victor Farias, *Heidegger and Nazism*, 1985 [1989]. In this (fairly anecdotal) book, we see how Heidegger fell prey, for a whole stretch of time, to a simulacrum. He thought he was upholding the event of his own thought.

6. [Badiou does not *always* use the term 'réel' in a strict Lacanian sense. *Translator's note.*]

7. Philippe Lacoue-Labarthe and Jean-Luc Nancy, *The Literary Absolute*, 1978 [1988]. These two authors have worked for years on the filiation between German Romanticism and the

aestheticization of politics in fascism. See also Lacoue-Labarthe's *Heidegger, Art and Politics*, 1988 [1990].

8. Alain Badiou, *Conditions*, 1992. There are two texts on the unnameable in this collection: 'Lecture on Subtraction', and 'Truth: Forcing and the Unnameable'.

9. Kurt Gödel, 'On Formally Undecidable Propositions of *Principia Mathematica* and Related Systems', in *Collected Works*, i, 145–95. It is important to understand *exactly* what this famous theorem says.

Conclusion

I began this book with a radical critique of 'ethical' ideology and its socialized variants: the doctrine of human rights, the victimary conception of Man, humanitarian interference, bio-ethics, shapeless 'democratism', the ethics of differences, cultural relativism, moral exoticism, and so on.

I tried to show that these intellectual tendencies of our time were at best variations on ancient religious and moral preaching, at worst a threatening mix of conservatism and the death drive.

We have identified, in that current of opinion which incessantly evokes 'ethics', a severe symptom of renunciation of the one thing that distinguishes the human species from the predatory living organism that it also is: the capacity to enter into the composition and becoming of some eternal truths.

From this point of view, I do not hesitate to say that 'ethical' ideology is, in our Western societies, the principal (albeit transitory) adversary of all those striving to hold fast to some true thought, whatever it be.

I then went on to sketch the reconstruction of an acceptable concept of ethics, whose maxim is subordinate to the development of truths. This maxim proclaims, in its general version, 'Keep going!' Continue to be this 'some-one', a human animal among others, which nevertheless finds itself *seized* and *displaced* by the evental process of a truth. Continue to be the active part of that subject of a truth that you have happened to become.

It is at the heart of the paradoxes provoked by this maxim that we discover the veritable figure of Evil (which in this way is dependent upon the Good, i.e. upon truths) in its three forms: the *simulacrum* (to be the terrorizing follower of a false event); *betrayal* (to give up on a truth in the name of one's interest); the forcing of the unnameable, or *disaster* (to believe in the total power of a truth).

So Evil is possible only through an encounter with the Good. The ethic of truths – which simply serves to lend consistency to that 'some-one' that we are, and which must manage to sustain, with its own animal perseverance, the intemporal perseverance of a subject of truth – is also that which tries to ward off Evil, through its effective and tenacious inclusion in the process of a truth.

This ethics combines, then, under the imperative to 'Keep going!', resources of discernment (do not fall for simulacra), of courage (do not give up), and of moderation [*réserve*] (do not get carried away to the extremes of Totality).

The ethic of truths aims neither to submit the world to the abstract rule of a Law, nor to struggle against an external and radical Evil. On the contrary, it strives, through its own fidelity to truths, to ward off Evil – that Evil which it recognizes as the underside, or dark side, of these very truths.

Appendix

══════ Appendix ══════

Politics and Philosophy: An Interview with Alain Badiou[1]

I

Peter Hallward: I thought we might begin with questions about politics – the place of the state, the relation between politics and economics on the one hand, and politics and culture on the other – and then go on to broader, more strictly philosophical questions – the relations between your mathematical ontology and material reality, between knowledge and truth, and among a plurality of subjects. To start, then, with the most pressing question of the moment: how has your understanding of politics changed since the late 1970s – that is, since the end of the Maoist intervention in France?

Alain Badiou: I think the first thing to change was our position concerning the status of the political party. Up to the end of the 1970s, my friends and I defended the idea that an emancipatory politics presumed some kind of political party. Today we are developing a completely different idea, which we call 'politics without party'. This doesn't mean 'unorganized politics'. All politics is collective, and so organized one way or another. 'Politics without party' means that politics does not spring from or originate in the party. It does not stem from that synthesis of theory and practice that represented, for Lenin, the Party. Politics springs from real situations, from what we can say and do in these situations. And so in reality there are political sequences, political processes, but these are not totalized by a party that would be simultaneously the representation of certain social forces and the source of politics itself.

And when you say: 'It is especially necessary to hold firmly to the prescriptions of L'Organisation Politique, whether it is a matter of the public services, of the factories, of the sans-papiers *[unregistered immigrants without residence papers], of the* foyers ouvriers *[workers' hostels] . . .*[2] *How do we resist an eventual institutionalization?*

I think it's possible to conceive and practise a discipline that is the discipline of the particular process itself. When we say, 'hold to the prescriptions,' these prescriptions are always relative to a concrete situation. They are singular prescriptions; they are neither ideological nor expressive of a party line. To give an example: if today we are grappling with the question of the *sans-papiers*, then what we call a prescription is so with regard to this precise question, itself caught up with the process of mobilization, of building a movement, and so on. There is certainly an element of discipline here. But it is not so much an organizational discipline, which we have neither the means nor the intention of consolidating, but simply a discipline of *thought.* If we are engaged in a process, engaged in the name of a certain number of statements, then the very existence of politics depends on a certain tenacity, a certain consistency.

The second thing that has changed over these last twenty years concerns the status of class. For a long time we were faithful to the idea of a class politics, a class state, and so on. Today we think that political initiatives which present themselves as representations of a class have given everything they had to give. The Marxist analysis of classes remains a fully reliable tool. I think that global trends have essentially confirmed some of Marx's fundamental intuitions. There is no going back on this; there is no need for a revision of Marxism itself. It is a matter of going beyond the idea that politics *represents* objective groups that can be designated as classes. This idea has had its power and importance. But in our opinion, we cannot today begin from or set out from this idea. We can begin from political processes, from political oppositions, from conflicts and contradictions, obviously. But it is no longer possible to code these phenomena in terms of representations of classes. In other words, emancipatory politics or reactionary politics may exist, but they cannot be rendered immediately transitive to a scientific, objective study of how class functions in society.

The third and final point of change concerns the state. We used to be convinced that a new political stage [*scène*] had to be built, a stage for the masses, that would be radically external or foreign to the mechanism of the state. We tended to leave the state outside of the field of politics in the strict sense. Politics unfolded according to the interests of the masses, and the state was the external adversary. This was our way of being faithful to the old communist idea of the withering away of the state, and of the state's necessarily bourgeois and reactionary character. Today our point of view is quite different. It is clear that there are two opposed forms of antistatism. There is the communist heritage of the withering of the state on the one hand; and on the other there is ultraliberalism, which also calls for the suppression of the state, or at least its reduction to its military and police functions. What we would say now is that there are a certain number of questions regarding which we cannot posit the absolute exteriority of the state. It is rather a matter of requiring something from the state, of formulating with respect to the state a certain number of prescriptions or statements. I'll take up the same example I gave a moment ago, because it is an example of militant urgency. Considering the fate of the *sans-papiers* in this country, a first orientation might have been: they should revolt against the state. Today we would say that the singular form of their struggle is, rather, to create the conditions in which the state is led to change this or that thing concerning them, to repeal the laws that should be appealed, to take the measures of naturalization [*régularisation*] that should be taken, and so on. This is what we mean by *prescriptions against the state*. This is not to say that we participate in the state. We remain outside the electoral system, outside any party representation. But we include the state within our political field, to the extent that, on a number of essential points, we have to work more through prescriptions against the state than in any radical exteriority to the state.

Is there a risk that such non-participant prescription might condemn itself to a marginal irresponsibility? Why is the party option so obviously obsolete? Why not support a party whose principles include, for example, the immediate legalization or naturalization of workers without residence papers?

Because today, parties are internal to the parliamentary state. It's simply not true that you can participate in a system as powerful and as ramified as parliamentarism without a real subjective commitment to it. In any case, the facts speak for themselves. *None* of the parties which have engaged in the parliamentary system and won governing power has escaped what I would call the subjective law of 'democracy', which is, when all is said and done, what Marx called an 'authorized representative' of capital. And I think that this is because, in order to participate in electoral or governmental representation, you have to conform to the subjectivity it demands – that is, a principle of continuity, the principle of the *politique unique*[3] – the principle of 'this is the way it is, there is nothing to be done', the principle of Maastricht, of a Europe in conformity with the financial markets, and so on. In France we've known this for a long time, for again and again, when left-wing parties come to power, they bring with them the themes of disappointment, broken promises, and so forth. I think we need to see this as an inflexible law, not as a matter of corruption. I don't think it happens because people change their minds, but because parliamentary subjectivity compels it.

So we must keep our distance from this subjective figure of politics. For us this means, concretely: don't stand for election, don't vote, don't expect anything from any political party. Which in no way excludes the creation of those conditions that might compel those within the parliamentary system to take a particular decision. Even regarding the question of the *sans-papiers*, if we consider the great movement to occupy the Saint Bernard church,[4] well, as far as the occupants are concerned, they have, by and large, received their residence papers. After being told no, they were told yes – without, as today's discussions show, any real change in the laws or the legal perspective. It was done because the new conditions required it to be done.

Before moving to the question of how then we might engage with capital directly, I'd like to ask you about L'Organisation Politique, which is still pretty unknown in Britain. Very briefly, what is it, and what does it do?

The core of L'Organisation Politique is made up of militants who have had a long history together, beginning with the events of May 1968 – in particular, Natacha Michel, Sylvain Lazarus, and myself. At the time, our engagement was organized around a very particular Marxist–Leninist– Maoist thematics. The story of French Maoism is very complicated, and I won't tell it here. L'Organisation Politique was created when we began to see things in a different way, regarding the questions of party, class, and state. The main orientations of L'Organisation Politique were established from around 1984–85, and we've now been publishing our journal, *La Distance politique,* for five or six years. Our work has focused on two principal sets of questions. The first concerns the realm of prescriptions against the state, which today turn on the issues of the *foyers ouvriers* and the set of questions relating to nationality and the status of foreigners: how do we count foreign workers in this country, do we count them for nothing or for something, and so on? This question is linked to the struggle against the [French] Front National. This domain of militant intervention has also concerned questions of equality in education and health, and so on.

Our second major focus concerns the status of factories, the possibility that politics takes root in or becomes stable through factories and places of work. We continue to see this as a decisive question, because it provides a kind of stable foundation to popular organization. So on the one hand we are working to establish directly political groups of workers in the factory, promoting a new figure of the worker, and on the other, to create new conditions concerning prescription against the state.

Roughly how many people are there in your group?

Very few. A few dozen genuine militants, capable of leading a political process. Personally, given the conditions of the moment, this doesn't much bother me. To know what people do is more important than knowing how many they are. In some situations, two people can do quite a lot where forty others might do very little. And it is true that in our own eyes, our political activity has something experimental about it. Unlike the political parties, we're not looking for institutional power. We are experimenting with what we can do in particular processes, which is a matter of meticulously detailed work. It is a matter of developing a different figure of politics from the figure of the revolutionary Party, as it has dominated things since October 1917. The experimental dimension is inevitable.

What is your relation to democracy as such? Your group maintains that 'the principle of democracy [is] that every-one counts as one'.[5] *But you don't vote, you don't participate.*

Democracy doesn't exactly mean that all individuals are counted as one in their own right. It's a matter of knowing how we are counted by the state. It's not the same thing. This question of democracy is profoundly linked to the state in general. Lenin used to say that ultimately, democracy is a kind of state. The question is how people are counted by the state. Are they counted equally? Are some counted less than others, or hardly counted at all? And what is counted needn't only be individuals. We can describe perfectly well how the state today counts workers without residence papers. In the case of factory organization, how does the employer count the workers' time, the time spent in the factory? It is a matter of asking how things in society are counted, or go uncounted. It is through this kind of question that, in our opinion, democracy exists as a real and active figure, and not merely as a juridical, constitutional mechanism.

One of the obvious virtues of your position regarding the sans-papiers *is that it separates very clearly the question of immigration from the very different question of unemployment. But by preserving the figure of the worker as the essential figure of immigration, is there a risk of reconnecting these two questions? And how can you avoid the directly economic pressure that has come to bear on the organization and location of factories over the last few decades? How can you maintain a political prescription on this point, without organizing a massive and specifically economic intervention?*

The figure of work and the figure of the worker are not at all the same. When we speak of a figure of the worker, it is not at all an economic figure, but a political one. In France, this question has a long history. We maintain that, over the last twenty years, there has been a systematic campaign to eliminate any figure of the worker from political space. 'Immigrant' is a word that came to be used at a certain moment in this campaign. For example, one of the first Mitterrand governments, the Mauroy government, during major workers' strikes at Flins, at Citroën, at Talbot, said that these workers were in fact immigrants, who were not really integrated into French social reality. The category 'immigrant' has been systematically substituted for the category 'worker', only to be supplanted in its turn by the category of the 'clandestine' or illegal alien. First workers, then immigrants, finally illegal aliens. If we insist that we are actually talking about workers – and whether they have worked, are working, or no longer work, doesn't represent a subjective difference – it is to struggle against this unceasing effort to erase any political reference to the figure of the worker. It is essential to ask whether, in politics, we count the figure of the worker for something, or for nothing. To count it for nothing means that we count nothing but capital. What is counted is the level of the stock market, the Euro, financial investment, competition, and so on; the figure of the worker, on the other hand, counts for nothing.

The question is all the more important in that it touches on much of the meaning of the December 1995 strikes in France. People protested: 'We don't count, the figure of work that we represent counts for nothing.' That's why we maintain that a figure of the worker – which does not mean a working class, or a charismatic proletariat – must be upheld as alive and active in the field of politics. And I think that this has nothing to do with those arguments that try to link the question of immigrants to a purely economic understanding of the amount of available work.

One last question about immigration. You describe it as a 'problem of internal politics', and distance yourselves from those who 'brandish pseudo-prescriptions, like the suppression of frontiers'.[6] *But doesn't a politics of unconditional naturalization remain pretty abstract, as long as current borders remain intact?*

I would say of the abolition of frontiers what I said a moment ago about the withering away of the state. I'm for it, I'm absolutely for it! But to be for something yields no active political principle in the situation. In reality, politics must always find its point of departure in the concrete situation. The question of knowing what happens to people who are in France is already a huge question. To refer this question back to a debate about the opening or the closing of borders, to the question of whether labour belongs to a global market or not, and so on, seems to forbid thinking about the situation itself and intervening in it so as to transform it.

The guiding principle concerning these questions should be as follows. We still belong to a historical era dominated by states and borders. There is nothing to suggest that this situation is going to change completely in the near future. The real question is whether the regulations [*réglementation*] at issue are more or less consistent with egalitarian aspirations. We should first tackle the question of how, concretely, we treat the people who are here; then, how we deal with those who would like to be here; and finally, what it is about the situation of their original countries that makes them want to leave. All three questions must be addressed, but in that order. To proclaim the slogan 'An end to frontiers' defines no real policy, because no one knows exactly what it means. Whereas by addressing the questions of how we treat the people who are here, who want to be here, or who find themselves obliged to leave their homes, we can initiate a genuine political process.

Let's move on to the more general question of the relation between the political and the economic. It's a little strange to run into a Marxist philosopher who rarely refers to the mode of production and some kind of economic determinism, however attenuated. Is there any danger that your relative silence on this score condemns you to what Lucien Goldmann used to call a 'tragic' condition – that is, a condition cut off from the real mechanisms of power that shape society?

The part of Marxism that consists of the scientific analysis of capital remains an absolutely valid background. After all, the realization of the world as global market, the undivided reign of great financial conglomerates, and so forth – all this is an indisputable reality and one that conforms, essentially, to Marx's analysis. The question is: where does politics fit in with all this? I think what is Marxist, and also Leninist – and in any case *true* – is the idea that any viable campaign against capitalism can only be political. There can be no economic battle against the economy. We have economist friends who analyse and criticize very well the existing systems of domination. But everything suggests that on this point, such knowledge is useful, but provides no answer by itself. The position of politics relative to the economy must be rethought, in a dimension that isn't really transitive. We don't simply fall, by successive representations, from the economy into politics. What kind of politics is *really* hetero-geneous to what capital demands? – that is today's question. Our politics is situated at the heart of things, in the factor-ies, in a direct relation with employers and with capital. But it remains a matter of politics – that is to say, of thought, of statements, of practices. All the efforts to construct an alternative economy strike me as pure and simple abstrac-tions, if not simply driven by the unconscious vector of capital's own reorganization. We can see, for example – and will see more and more – how so many environmentalist demands simply provide capital with new fields of invest-ment, new inflections and new deployments. Why? Because every proposition that directly concerns the economy can be assimilated by capital. This is so by definition, since capital is indifferent to the qualitative configuration of things. So long as it can be transformed or aligned in terms of market value, everything's fine.

The only strategy worth the name is a political struggle – that is to say, a singular, active subjectivity, a thought-praxis [*pensée-pratique*]. We are in the phase of experimentation.

And the Cuban situation, for instance?

I respect Cuba as a figure of resistance, for we should respect all the forms of resistance to the hegemony of the global market, and to its principal organizer: American imperialism. But Cuba provides singular testimony of an outmoded conception of politics. And so Cuba will have, unavoidably, very serious problems, internal problems, because it bears witness, with incontestable grandeur, to a figure of the Party–State that belongs to another political age. Everything that exists is born, develops and comes to an end. After which we move on to something else.

What about the relation between politics and culture? One of the most immediately striking things about your work, perhaps especially for Anglophone readers, is your hostility to the contemporary consensus on questions of liberal-democratic procedure, human rights, and our much-vaunted respect for cultural difference. We might cite the recent works of Habermas, Rorty, and Charles Taylor, as much as Luc Ferry and Alain Renaut – but even in the French domain, we would have to relate the questions raised by the so-called nouvelle philosophie *back to the apparent 'ethical turn' of Lyotard (through Kant) and Derrida (through Lévinas), as much as of the last works of Foucault. Where do you stand in relation to the contemporary obsession with the 'other', with the valorization of difference as such? How do you avoid this question, once it's been admitted that it is not a matter of claiming a particular essence (sexual, racial or religious), but of developing a critical position that takes account of the fact that where people are oppressed, they are oppressed as women, as black, as Jewish or Arab. . . .*

When I hear people say 'We are oppressed as blacks, as women', I have only one problem: what exactly is meant by 'black' or 'women'? If this or that particular identity is put into play in the struggle against oppression, against the state, my only problem is with the exact political meaning of the identity being promoted. Can this identity, in itself, function in a progressive fashion – that is, other than as a property invented by the oppressors themselves? In his preface to *Les nègres*, Jean Genet said that everything turns around the question: what are black people, and for starters, what colour are they? You can answer then that black people are black. But what does 'black' mean to those who, in the name of the oppression they suffer, make it a political category? I understand very well what black means for those who use that predicate in a logic of differentiation, oppression, and separation. Just as I understand very well what 'French' means when Le Pen uses the word, when he champions national preference, France for the French, exclusion of Arabs, and so on. If someone wants to use the words 'French' or 'Arab' in another way, to inscribe them in a progressive political affirmation, everything depends on what this determination then means for the person who uses it. And what it means *for everyone*, what it means universally.

'*Négritude*', for example, as incarnated by Césaire and Senghor, consisted essentially of reworking exactly those traditional predicates once used to designate black people: as intuitive, as natural, as primitive, as living by rhythm rather than by concepts, and so on. It's no accident that it was a primarily poetic operation, a matter of turning these predicates upside down, of claiming them as affirmative and liberating. I understand why this kind of movement took place, why it was necessary. It was a very strong, very beautiful, and very necessary movement. But having said that, it is not something that can be inscribed as such in politics. I think it is a matter of poetics, of culture, of turning the subjective situation upside down. It doesn't provide a possible framework for political initiative.

The progressive formulation of a cause which engages cultural or communal predicates, linked to incontestable situations of oppression and humiliation, presumes that we propose these predicates, these particularities, these singularities, these communal qualities, in such a way that they be situated in another space and become heterogeneous to their ordinary oppressive operation. I never know in advance what quality, what particularity, is capable of becoming political or not; I have no preconceptions on that score. What I do know is that there must be a progressive meaning to these particularities, a meaning that is intelligible to all. Otherwise, we have something which has its *raison d'être*, but which is necessarily of the order of a demand for integration – that is, of a demand that one's particularity be valued in the existing state of things. This is something commendable, even necessary, but it is not, in my opinion, something to be inscribed directly in politics. Rather, it inscribes itself in what I would generally call 'syndicalism' [trade unionism] – that is to say, *particular* claims, claims that seek to be recognized and valued in a determinate relation of forces. I would call 'political' something that – in the categories, the slogans, the statements it puts forward – is less the demand of a social fraction or community to be integrated into the existing order than something which touches on a transformation of that order as a whole.

A last example on this point: what is the legitimate political usage of the category 'Jew'? It is very hard to ask this question in France, without instantly being labelled an anti-Semite. I think, though, that it is absolutely necessary, if this word is to have a progressive political signification, that it be something different from what Hitler, for instance, designated by that name. It can't be the same thing *turned on its head.* And if it is something else, we have to ask what it might be – what relation it has or doesn't have with the state of Israel and its practices, what relation it has or doesn't have with religion, with the matrilineal character of Judaism, or with the revolutionary engagement of so many Jews in the 1930s and 1940s, and so forth.

But surely most of the historical answers to this question have included an element of irreducible particularity, a constitutive particularization, we might say; how to describe what the word 'Jew' means without referring to the theme of the chosen?

That there is a remnant, or a support [*support*], of irreducible particularity, is in fact something I would acknowledge for any kind of reality. To take up again the most urgent example in France today: it is perfectly obvious that the *sans-papiers* of the *foyers* [workers' hostels] are very particular – they are not simply Africans, but mainly from Mali, and often from a particular area in Mali. They practise a whole series of transpositions of village customs in their way of living in the *foyers*. They maintain a strong relation to their traditional hierarchy. When you attend a *foyer* meeting, you immediately notice that the meeting takes place in a particular way. But in the end, between this particularity present in the practical, concrete support of any political process, and the statements in the name of which the political process unfolds, I think there is only a relation of support, but not a relation of transitivity. It's a bit like the relation with the economy. You can't go from the one to the other, even if one seems to be 'carried' by the other.

So to take up the question of the meaning of the word 'Jew', it follows the same logic. Of course I recognize the consistency of the historical particularity covered by this word. But it in no way settles the question of in what sense the term can become a political category. I don't say that it can't happen, or that it shouldn't happen. But something more than this particularity would be necessary for it to happen. Because I know very well that people try to legitimate things in the name of this particularity that I condemn absolutely, like supporting the action of the state of Israel, as well as things that I support, like the effort of some Israelis to develop positive relations with the Palestinians. In each case we have to work to make a category pass from what I called its identitarian or syndical status to a political status.

Most of the verbs you usually use to describe the passage from particular to universal, however, are verbs like subtract, extract, depose. . . . Can we progress, by essentially negative or subtractive means, to a point where once-despised particularities can attain a universal signification? You suggest that things like 'the language we choose to speak, the things we eat, the people we marry and love, our customs and habits, all this changes, without strictly speaking anyone's intervention'.[7] the history of colonization, however, to mention only that, suggests otherwise.

As I said, I think the moment of turning things upside down is inevitable. And obviously, for example, the questions of language, of history, of national singularity, are genuinely political questions for countries which are struggling against a colonizer, or countries which have recently emerged from colonization. But we have to recognize that they are ultimately political only because the historical movement for popular and national liberation against imperialism carried a certain universality. In the 1960s it was – especially for the youth of the world – a major cause. Today we see clearly that everything depends on the clarity of the categories put into play; their political character is not obvious. I think, for example, that the demonization of the figure of Islam by the Western powers, and especially in France, is certainly reactionary. But this doesn't mean – unlike the case of the people's struggle in Vietnam, or the national struggle in Algeria – that the political and universalizable character of what is at stake on this point is fully transparent. It isn't. It may become so, as everything begins in confusion and obscurity, but it isn't yet. My feeling is that we are at the beginning of a new era. At the level of world history, this new era has been massively marked by the collapse of the USSR – a major historical settling of accounts [*une échéance historique majeure*] – and consequently, a new period of American hegemony. As so often happens, progressive thought has fallen behind all this.

To conclude on this point, and to make sure that there is no ambiguity, I want to underline the fact that no category is *in itself* blocked from its possible politicization. Even 'Arab', even 'Islam', even 'Jew', even 'French', can, at a given moment, have a progressive political signification. When de Gaulle addressed the French from London – the French meaning, for him, the resistants – 'French' had a progressive signification, that of anti-Nazi resistance. This proves that these things can change. On the other hand, I would say that it is never given in advance; it is not because a term is a communal predicate, nor even because there is a victim in a particular situation, that it is automatically, or even easily, transformed into a political category.

A final question on this issue: in your book on Saint Paul you distinguish between the logic of capital on the one hand, taking cultural identities and differences as its currency, and on the other, the logic of a truth which 'deposes differences', which 'seeks new

differences, new particularities in which to expose the universality'
of the truth.[8] *Isn't this second logic, the logic of deposing and*
exposing, as close as the first to what Marx describes as the process
of reification, the investing of the dead matter of obsolete differences
with the exclusively animating force of capital itself?

Emancipatory politics, as I say somewhere in my *Manifesto
for Philosophy*, must be at least equal to the challenge of
capital. That is Marx's idea. When Marx says that capital
destroys all the old ties, all the ancient sacred figures, that
it dissolves everything in the frozen waters of selfish calculation, he says it with a certain admiration.[9] Marx had
already distinguished himself from those who dreamed
nostalgically of a resistance to capital rooted in ancient
customs and territories. He called this reactive phenomenon 'feudal socialism'. Marx was radically critical of this
idea, and this is because he accepted that there were formal
similarities between the ambitions of emancipatory politics
and the workings of capital. Because we can never go back
on universalism. There is no earlier territoriality calling for
protection or recovery. The whole point is that differences
be traversed, conserved and deposed simultaneously, somewhere other than in the frozen waters of selfish calculation.
Obviously it's a formidably complex problem, which can
sometimes expose us, I admit, to the risk of being the
unconscious agents of capital itself. I remember the days
when the French progressive movement – and Deleuze was
very engaged in this – supported the creation of free [i.e.
private-sector] radio stations. At the time, French radio was
still entirely state-run. The creation of free radio stations
was to be the conquest of a fragmented, multiform territoriality. And Deleuze was partly right. But for the most

part, what took place, overwhelmingly, was the conquest of radio by capital. This is always the danger. We can't avoid it. Because on this point we are rivals to capital, rather than merely reacting against it. It is a struggle of universalism against universalism, not of particularism against universalism.

Following André Gorz, lots of people have said farewell to the working class, so as to support – perhaps with a certain idealism – the category of 'new social movements'. I'm thinking of Touraine, of Laclau and Mouffe, even of Foucault. What do you make of this trend?

We are entirely opposed to it. Certainly, the great critique of 'classism' undertaken by my friend Sylvain Lazarus demonstrates that we know how a certain vision of class politics has been saturated. We don't say that it has failed. It has given what it had to give. It has been a great enterprise [*expérience*], with its darkness, its terrors, but also with its extraordinary creative enthusiasms and its ability, after all, here and there, to strike real blows against imperialism. This time has come to an end, and so we can say, if you like, that the category of the proletariat, as a political category, can no longer play much of a role.

But in terms of what they propose, I think that in camouflaged form, the abandon promoted by Gorz and others in fact shows that they have been won over, politically, to the established order. It leaves the properly political sphere untouched. It represents a kind of idealization of a self-regulating social movement of capital itself. It is a vision of the affluent: the rich societies' dream of a maximum possible comfort. And so we are to busy ourselves with the environment, with development, with the reduction of the working week, with recreation, with education [*formation*] for all. I'd accept your characterization of this trend: I see in it a fairly feeble idealism, and a veritable renunciation of politics as independent thought-praxis.

And the figure of Hannah Arendt, the great renewal of interest in her work over the last few years? For she, not unlike you, insists on the strict demarcation of the political from the cultural or economic, and insists in particular on the importance of 'deliberate beginnings' in politics.[10] *But I wonder if she might find in your work traces of a kind of totalitarianism, of the belief that in some sense 'everything is possible'.*

The conception of politics that we defend is far from the idea that 'everything is possible'. In fact, it's an immense task to try to propose a few possibles, in the plural – a few possibilities other than what we are told is possible. It is a matter of showing how the space of the possible is larger than the one we are assigned – that something else is possible, but not that everything is possible. In any case, it is essential that politics renounce the category of totality, which is perhaps another change with respect to the previous period.

The real difference with Hannah Arendt should, rather, be located in her definition of politics itself. For Arendt, politics concerns 'living together', the regulation of being together as a republic, or as public space. It's not an adequate definition. It reduces politics to the sole instance of judgement, and eventually to opinion, rather than recognizing that the essence of politics concerns thought and action, as connected through the practical consequences of a prescription. For any one prescription is opposed to others. There can be no homogeneous public space other than that of consensus – the consensus we are all familiar with, the consensus of *la pensée unique* [i.e. global liberalism]. I've always been struck by the fact that Hannah Arendt prefers the American Constitution to the French Revolution. I don't say this out of chauvinism, but because I think these are two important historical images. On the one hand, the constitutional creation of a complex, ramified public space, elaborated in detail down to the finer points concerning the election of judges. On the other hand, something sequential, something more antagonistic, and more principled. I stand resolutely for the second option.

This brings me to one of my main questions, the question of the plurality of subjects – if to be subject means to be the subject of (or to) a truth. In your Saint Paul, *for example, you generally speak of 'the Christian subject'. How do we preserve the militant unity of a group of subjects, other than in the Jacobin manner, other than through the imposition of an eventual orthodoxy? How can the saint avoid eventually becoming a priest? What sort of space is there in your philosophy for subjective disagreement?*

Let's not forget that I conceive of a truth not as a pre-given transcendent norm, in the name of which we are supposed to act, but as a *production*. At a certain moment, the set of actors of a generic procedure, of a truth-procedure, are clearly ignorant, unknowing, of what it is. This is an essential point. So nobody is in a position to say that since he *knows* the truth, he is the one who will decree [*normer*] how it is to be known, since the truth itself depends on its own production.

The only thing we have to question are the conditions of this production. I'm convinced that in politics, for example, it is very largely deliberative. There is no reason why it should be Jacobin or terrorist. The Jacobin terror had its roots not in internal disagreement, but in the situation of crisis, the war and the counter-revolution. As a general rule, every generic procedure is in reality a process that can perfectly well be deliberative, as long as we understand that it invents its rule of deliberation at the same time as it invents itself. And it is no more constrained by a pre-established norm that follows from the rule of deliberation. You have only to look at how the rule of deliberation in different organizations, in different political sequences, and in different political modes, is entirely variable. For example – to take only one story, and only a couple of sequences in this story – it is entirely different under Lenin and under Stalin. Under Lenin, there were some absolutely dramatic disagreements. On a question as essential as that of whether or not to launch the insurrection, Lenin was in radical opposition to Zinoviev, Kamenev, and many others. In the end, a protocol of decision-making was found that didn't involve the extermination of opposing views. Under Stalin, by contrast, such extermination practically becomes the rule. Every time a plurality of individuals, a plurality of human subjects, is engaged in a process of truth, the construction of this process induces the construction of a deliberative and collective figure of this production, which is itself variable.

If subjects exist only in the fidelity to the truth they proclaim, how do we avoid the eventual and potentially oppressive measurement

of the relative authenticity or intensity of this fidelity – the judge-
ment of subjects as more or less close to the pure truth? That this
truth is in a sense unknowable doesn't simplify the question.

There is no difficulty *of principle* in accepting the fact that
within a plurality of human subjects, there exist differences
of more and less. It's inevitable. The only problem is
in knowing how these differences are normed [*normées*],
ruled, and above all, how this is related to the production
of the successive stages of the sequence in question. To take
the restricted example of love, which engages two people,
the smallest possible plurality: everyone knows that every
disagreement needn't lead automatically to a break-up. At
the same time, each figure of love invents and elaborates,
over the course of its development, the regime of its dis-
putes. Obviously, in some cases, there are break-ups. But in
others there aren't. And the way in which the productive or
creative positivity of this love is articulated with the internal
regulation of disagreement simply defines *one* of the singularities of its trajectory.

The same goes for politics. The dialectic of 'more or less'
regulates a certain form of collective deliberation or collective engagement, but needn't drive things toward a binary
logic. I would say – to use an algebraic metaphor – that it
needn't present itself as a logic with two values. Everyone
can accept the existence of intermediary nuances. Mao
himself – and God knows there was a great deal of violence
in the Chinese Revolution – developed a fairly complicated
doctrine regarding the difference between contradictions
among the people and antagonistic contradictions, and the
existence in any process of left, centre, and right wings. He
never stopped insisting that in the movement of a process

there is always a considerable plurality of nuances, and that if we don't grant some space to this plurality, we are finally driven back to the break-up of the process, more than anything else. It is true that some political sequences did adopt as the internal rule of their development a very severe bivalent logic, but we need to ask in each case how this bivalence was linked to the singularity of the sequence. It is not a general problem of truth-processes.

II

I'd like to turn now to more strictly philosophical questions, beginning with Plato. Along with a few others – Guy Lardreau and Christian Jambet in particular – you declare a fairly unusual fidelity to Plato. Why? What does Platonism mean, once you have renounced its transcendent aspect?

I wouldn't say that there is no transcendent dimension in Plato, but it's not what interests me, it's not why I align myself with him, in slightly provocative fashion – since all the major philosophical figures of the past century, from Nietzsche through Heidegger, have been anti-Platonists.

In fact, three things about Plato interest me. First, his sharp, inaugural awareness of what I call the 'conditions' of philosophy. Philosophy is to be found in obligatory dialogue with mathematics, with art and poetry – even if this dialogue is strained and difficult; with politics, and also with love, as demonstrated in the *Symposium* and other dialogues. This is a long way from the idea that philosophy is a total knowledge or system. For Plato, philosophy begins thinking not in relation to itself but in relation to something else – to the people you meet and what they say (Socrates), but also, in relation to the discoveries of the mathematicians, to the work of those who write poetry and tragedy, to political situations and debates, to the existence and intensity of the feeling of love.

The second thing that interests me is Plato's conviction that philosophy doesn't add up to very much without the category of truth. This is my antimodern or anticontemporary aspect – for this category is suspected, criticized, that is, denied, by most contemporary trends. I would even say that philosophy means little without the idea that there can be eternal truths. . . . Of course this idea is present in the whole of classical metaphysics, but in Plato, it remains somewhat questioning and fragmentary. The question animates most of the dialogues, but it is nevertheless very hard to find a closed theory of truth in them, because it is always taken up again, in new conditions, with regard to something else. This suits me as a philosopher, this rhythm, in which we place ourselves under the sign of the question of truth even as we recognize that it can never be the object of a self-sufficient or complete demonstration.

Finally, I think there is a Plato who is interested not at all in the transcendence of the Ideas, but in what we might call – to use one of Heidegger's titles – the question 'what is thinking?' We will naturally name what is thinkable, what there is in thought, Idea. But – especially in the later dialogues: the *Sophist*, the *Parmenides*, the *Philebus* – Plato doesn't pose the question 'what is thought?' by any means to privilege a transcendence but, rather, to ask: what is an internal articulation between Ideas, what is the movement of thought, what is its internal alterity, its impasse, and so on? For me, this is Plato.

*And 'your master Lacan'? What do you retain from his teaching
today? Did you attend his seminar?*

I've actually always kept myself at quite a distance from
Lacan. I never attended his seminar, but at the same time,
I was first, with Althusser, to present reports on his work at
the Ecole Normale Supérieure (1958–59). I have never had
any relation to the practice of psychoanalysis. I am neither
analyst nor analysand, nor analysed, nor am I a member of
any Lacanian school. My relation to Lacan is internal to
philosophy.

That said, I've learned a number of important things
from Lacan, and that's why I consider him to be one of my
masters. To put it briefly, what fascinated me about Lacan
for a long time was his very strange effort to link the
question of the subject to investigations or models of a
logico-mathematical kind. This effort is totally absent from
Freud. What especially interested me about Lacan was his
conception of the real. First, the distinction he makes
between the real and reality, which is not the same as the
classical metaphysical distinction between appearance and
reality, or between phenomenon and noumenon. And in
particular, this conception of the real as being, in a situation, in any given symbolic field, the point of impasse, or
the point of impossibility, which precisely allows us to think
the situation as a whole, according to its real. Part of what I
said a moment ago could be resaid as follows: emancipatory
politics always consists in making seem possible precisely
that which, from within the situation, is declared to be
impossible.

Another thing that grabbed my attention: Lacan declared
himself to be an 'antiphilosopher'. It is partly thanks to him

that I began to ask myself, in a fairly systematic way, what might be declared antiphilosophical, what was it that characterized antiphilosophical thought, why certain kinds of thought constitute themselves as hostility to philosophy. In the end, my theory is that philosophy should always think as closely as possible to antiphilosophy. For all these reasons, I owe Lacan a real debt, despite having had no relation to the question of analytic therapy as such.

You are careful to distinguish philosophical truth from all that might claim an affinity with the ineffable, the unsayable, or the mystical. At the same time, you defend, in Saint Paul *and elsewhere, a striking doctrine of 'laicized grace', purged of any religious reference or thematics. The question is: doesn't the truly religious begin precisely where all thematics comes to an end? What can the idea of grace mean, if it doesn't connote the idea of another, properly creative power, a pure beyond?*

For me, every singular truth has its origin in an event. Something must happen, in order for there to be something new. Even in our personal lives, there must be an encounter, there must be something which cannot be calculated, predicted or managed; there must be a break based only on chance. And it's to the extent that there is an essential link between the infinite development or construction of a truth, and this element of rupture that is an event, that I understand what Christian writers have called grace. That is not to say that for them the term has exactly this meaning. In effect, if every grace is a divine gift, we cannot absolutely avoid the idea of an ultimate, divine calculation, even if that calculation exceeds our understanding. That would be the difference that subsists between the properly religious understanding of grace, and what I call laicized grace.

Fundamentally, what I call laicized grace describes the fact that, in so far as we are given a chance of truth, a chance of being a little bit more than living individuals, pursuing our ordinary interests, this chance is always given to us through an event. This evental giving, based absolutely on chance, and beyond any principle of the management or calculation of existence – why not call it a grace? Simply, it is a grace that requires no all-powerful, no divine transcendence. What interests me in Saint Paul is the idea – very explicit in his writings – that the becoming of a truth, the becoming of a subject, depend entirely on a pure event, which is itself beyond all the predictions and calculations that our understanding is capable of.

What, then, do we make, with Paul, of that second and no less fundamental event, his personal confirmation, on the road to Damascus, of the truth of the first event? Is there room, in your philosophy, for this second and irreducibly private *supplement? In other words, is the truth not always split between a truth 'in general' or 'for all', and a truth reserved especially for its avant-garde? Or again, what is gained by distinguishing so sharply, in politics as much as in love, what happens to us from what we do, or make happen?*

What is important about Paul is that we can *read* the texts he left behind, quite independently of the story of his personal grace, and of the way this grace itself did or did not depend on the resurrection. Paul's thought is a thought of the event, a thought of the truth as consecutive to an event, a thought of fidelity, and also a certain thought of the universal, and what interested me was to examine it as such. That there are serious problems within Christian doctrine – concerning whether the event was sufficient or not, concerning who is chosen – is something that goes back to what we were saying: that it is very difficult to detach the Christian doctrine of grace from the idea of a transcendent plan that governs the world. Which is where my atheism interrupts the parallel, as I point out on several occasions in my book.

On the other hand, I don't see any major problem as regards the collective extension of an event, if only because I've lived through something like it myself. A philosophy is also a personal experience. Concerning May 1968 and after, you have to remember just what the established Gaullist regime was like in the early 1960s. You have to remember its oppressiveness, and the extraordinarily minoritarian character – in a way we can scarcely imagine today – of the protest movements, of radical or critical currents, confronted with the triumphalism of Pompidolian propertied capitalism. You need to have lived through that society, a society which had no more problems – the terrible question of Algeria having been resolved; a society of full employment, of uninterrupted development. . . . As for what then took place, yes, we were the genuine actors, but actors absolutely seized by what was happening to them, as by something extraordinary, something properly incalculable. Without a doubt, I was personally marked by this irruption. Of course, if we add up the anecdotes one by one, we can always say that at any given moment there were certain actors, certain people who provoked this or that result. But the crystallization of all these moments, their generalization, and then the way in which everyone was caught up in it, well beyond what any one person might have thought possible – that's what I call an evental dimension. *None* of the little processes that led to the event was equal to what actually took place.

It's a matter of scale?

There was an extraordinary change of scale, as there always is in every significant event. For example, between the French Revolution and the financial crisis that prompted the calling of the Estates General, there was another change of scale. Of course we can always invoke the meeting of the Estates General, the question of the representation of the different orders, the king's attempts to block all that. I've never argued that the event, when we examine it in its facticity, presents irrational characteristics. I simply think that none of the calculations internal to the situation can account for its irruption, and cannot, in particular, elucidate this kind of break in scale that happens at a certain moment, such that the actors themselves are seized by something of which they no longer know if they are its actors or its vehicle [*supports*], or what it carries away. Lin Piao – someone who is rarely mentioned these days – once said, at the height of the Cultural Revolution, that the essential thing was to be, at a revolutionary conjunction, both its actor and its target. I quite like this formula. Yes, we are actors, but in such a way that we are targeted by, carried away by, and struck by [*atteint par*] the event. In this sense there can undoubtedly be collective events.

You raise the example of Castro, who is dear to me because he's part of my youth. I followed what happened in Cuba very closely, and there again, it's obvious that the little

group of partisans in the Sierra Maestra were voluntarists.
But with the collapse of Batista, the seizure of power, and
that extraordinary, very slow march of Castro towards
Havana, the Cuban people as a whole were seized by
something which, in a certain way, was no doubt legible in
its successive stages, but which marked an absolute change
of scale with respect to the disembarkation of some twenty
people in the hills of the Sierra Maestra. . . .

You once said that you were no longer sure if there was an event in
May 1968.[11] *By what criteria can we decide such things after the*
event, especially if the event itself persists, strictly speaking, only
through its retrospective declaration?

I said something a little more complicated. I said that
perhaps we didn't know the name of this event, and that,
consequently, it was an event-ality still suspended from its
name – what Sylvain Lazarus calls an 'obscure eventality'.
There are such eventalities – that is, eventalities such that
the statements that can be detached from them, or the
names used to refer to them, never manage to justify the
practice of the sequence, never manage to stabilize it. For
example, in the French Revolutionary sequence, the name
'revolution' was very soon a matter of consensus, as the
appropriate name for what was going on. When Saint-Just
said: 'The revolution is frozen,' he pointed to something
about the Revolution and the name 'revolution', as a
capacity that was truly internal to what was going on at the
time.

As for May 1968, we've drifted this way and that, perhaps
because it is an event belonging to precisely that time when
we were passing from the old conception of politics to

something else, so that, as a result, the name 'revolution' wasn't the right name. There have been all sorts of proposals. I'm very struck by the fact that today everyone says 'the events of May 1968', but if we say that the event has 'event' as its name, it means that we haven't yet found its name. I expect that I will probably stick with this appreciation of May 1968: it is an event – part of my subjectivation was forged in it, so I will remain faithful to it – but one whose name is obscure.

One of the first questions to strike me as I read L'Etre et l'événement *was that of the general relation between your mathematical ontology and the nature of material reality in general. You treat material situations as particular sorts of mathematical sets. What relation is there between your ontology – that is, the presentation of presentation, what you call 'being-as-being' – and that which is presented?*

If we accept that there exists a situation in which what is at stake for thought is being-as-being – and for me, this is simply one situation of thought, among others – then I would say that this situation is the situation defined by mathematics. Mathematics, because if we abstract all presentative predicates little by little, we are left with the multiple, pure and simple. The 'that which is presented' can be absolutely anything. Pure presentation as such, abstracting all reference to 'that which' – which is to say, then, being-as-being, being as pure multiplicity – can be thought only through mathematics.

To the extent that we abstract the 'that which is presented' in the diversity of situations, to consider the presentation of presentation itself – that is to say, in the end, pure multiplicity

– then the real and the possible are rendered necessarily indistinct. What I call ontology is the generic form of presentation as such, considered independently of the question as to whether what is presented is real or possible. It is the reason why people have always debated the status of mathematical idealities, the status of their reality. Are they real, do they exist somewhere, are they merely possible, are they linguistic products . . .? I think we have to abandon these questions, simply because it is of the essence of ontology, as I conceive it, to be beneath the distinction of the real and the possible. What we will necessarily be left with is a science of the multiple in general, such that the question of knowing what is effectively presented in a particular situation remains suspended. *A contrario*, every time we examine something that is presented, from the strict point of view of its objective presentation, we will have a horizon of mathematicity, which is, in my opinion, the only thing that can be clear. In the final analysis, physics – that is to say, the theory of matter – is mathematical. It is mathematical because, as the theory of the most objectified strata of the presented as such, it necessarily catches hold of being-as-being through its mathematicity.

The relation between 'what is presented' – for example, matter – and the theory of being-as-being can be described, empirically, as the relation between physics and mathematics. But it might be described more profoundly as the relation between, on the one hand, a generic theory of the multiple in itself – that is, of a multiple indifferent to what it is the multiple of, and thus of the multiple as pure multiple of the multiple – and, on the other hand, the 'that which is multiply presented as such', about which ontology says nothing.

It seems, however, that your most basic concept, the concept of a
situation, *oscillates somewhat between an essentially mathematical*
order and what appears to be a no less essentially eclectic order,
combining heterogeneous elements of actuality.

You're quite right. The category of situation, from this point
of view – and this is why I'm going substantially to rework it
– is a bivalent category, a category we can access in two
different ways [*à double entrée*]. In one sense you can take it
to mean situation as effectivity – that is, as the effective
realization of an ontological possibility, and so as a figure
of multiplicity. This would be how it is characterized from
within the ontological situation. We could then say that
every situation is a multiple. We could further add that
every situation is an infinite multiple, or a multiple of such
and such a cardinality, or a multiple of such and such
complexity, and that would be about as far as we could go.
In a second sense, the 'that which composes this multiplicity', the qualitative determination internal to this multiplicity, will be a matter for the investigation of *this* singular
situation. We could say then, for instance, that it is a
politico-historical situation, made up of gestures, actions of
the masses, figures of the state, and so on. If, by contrast, it
is a strictly physical or material situation, it will be made up
of experimental mechanisms highlighting particular sets
[*ensembles*].

All this simply confirms a very old and somewhat inevitable ontological programme: that ontology always gathers
up what remains to thought once we abandon the predicative, particular determinations of 'that which is presented'.
We might conclude that there remains nothing at all. This
was the idea that dominated the whole nineteenth century,

the whole of post-Kantian theory, according to which, in this case, there would remain only the unknowable, and eventually nothing. Or we might conclude that there actually remains everything – which was, after all, Heidegger's guiding inspiration; that is, if we put to one side the diverse singularity of the existence of the existent [*étant*], we come to a thought of being that is itself suspended or deferred [*suspendue*] in fairly problematic fashion. As for me, I conclude that what remains is mathematics. I think it's a fairly strong thesis.

Moreover, it is a fully materialist thesis, because everyone can see that the investigation of matter, the very concept of matter, is a concept whose history shows it to be at the edge of mathematicity. It is not mathematical in the order of experience, but it is mathematized by rational thought – such that it is on the border of the mathematical, since the more you decompose the concept of matter into its most elementary constituents, the more you move into a field of reality which can be named or identified only with increasingly complex mathematical operations. 'Matter' would simply be, immediately after being, the most general possible name of the presented (of 'what is presented'). Being-as-being would be that point of indistinction between the possible and the real that only mathematics apprehends in the exploration of the general configurations of the purely multiple. Matter, in the sense in which it is at stake in physics, is matter as enveloping any particular presentation – and I am a materialist in the sense that I think that any presentation is material. If we consider the word 'matter', the content of the word 'matter', matter comes immediately after being. It is the degree of generality immediately co-present to ontology. The physical situation will then be a very powerfully mathematized situation, and in a certain sense, more and more so, the closer it comes to apprehending the smallest, most primordial elements of reality.

One of the consequences – or perhaps one of the conditions – of your position is to bracket the distinction which has so often inspired ontological inquiry: the distinction between the animate and inanimate, or between the living and the more-than-living, the distinction between the created and the Creator. Does your recourse to mathematics allow you to sidestep the old problems associated with our attempt to make sense of a reality that is not of the same order as our own experience?

I'm convinced of the importance of the situational field concerning the theory of living beings. I think that the theory of the living as living, like the theory of matter as matter, is a matter for science. And God knows I recognize the eminent dignity and singular importance of science among the conditions of philosophy. If I haven't yet said much about the field of the living, it's not at all because I think it's unnecessary. In any case, I have always said that we have to accept the fact that human beings are animals.

You're sometimes a little hard on animals. . . .

No! Why do you say that?

This effort to distinguish an immortal truth from the corruption of the flesh, of temptation, of desires and interests that are 'no more, no less worthy than those of moles. . . .'[12]

But let's make some distinctions. I do think there is a real difference between the human and the animal. This doesn't mean that I deny that, for the essential part of our existence, we are animals. I've often said as much. A major part of human existence is *grasped*, seized, within animal existence. This is not a value judgement, it just means that if we're going to talk about truth-procedures, we're going to talk about something else. This something else is what constitutes the singularly human, within the animal universe. Personally, I'm quite fascinated by everything that reminds me to what extent human beings are animals. I have a certain tenderness for this. I'm by no means the kind of classical moralist for whom the animality within the human is always the object of an initial prejudice. It's a part of my materialism.

I think that human beings are animals, animals which have at their disposal a singular ability, a singular, aleatory, and partial ability, which identifies them philosophically as human, within the animal sphere. The animal sphere is itself internal to the material sphere. From the point of view of the pure presented, it ends there. But where a thought of being is concerned – and it is precisely one of the singular human capacities – we have the use of mathematics.

You once accused me of being pre-Darwinian; this was an important objection in your view. It struck me, that remark, and I've thought about it. I have the greatest admiration for Darwin. His revolutionary discovery was a major creation in human thought. Bearing in mind the conditions of the day, his theory was very powerful, with remarkable subversive potential. It's not for nothing that it has always been the target of reactionary attacks. I don't think I am pre-Darwinian. I accept absolutely that man is an animal and, in a certain sense, nothing else. From the point of view of what composes us, there is nothing except matter. Even a procedure of truth is never anything other than the seizing of materiality.

Having said that, I do think that, *by grace*, this particular animal is sometimes seized by something that thought cannot manage to reduce strictly to the thought of animality as such. It is not a very different claim from the one a physicist will make by saying that, however mathematized physics becomes, there neverless remains a moment where it is experience or the experiment [*l'expérience*] which decides an issue, where everything is not reducible to that sole space exhaustively thought by pure mathematicity. As for truth, it's the same thing – that is to say, it is thinkable only by that mortal animal which human beings happen to be.

What then, exactly, is the relation between the immortality of the truth and the 'animality' of the knowledges it transcends? In the first place, we know that according to your ontology, the elements of a situation exist as 'counted-for-one' by the situation. Are they thus intrinsically individuated or self-individuated, and then selected by the situation? Or are they distinguished solely by their belonging to the situation? What distinguishes an element?

Your question puts you in a position of indiscernibility. We cannot immediately distinguish between the fact that an element is counted as one in the situation, and the one that it is 'in itself'. What can happen is that, in a manner that is itself unavoidably evental, some elements that were not previously counted, come to appear as needing to be

counted in the situation. It is only through this discovery
that there irrupts a gap between what is counted as one in
the situation, and the intrinsic one that the element is.
Retroactively, we will have to declare that this something
which appears, eventually, as needing to be counted – did
indeed belong to the situation. And if you admit retroactively that it belonged to the situation, you will have to say
that it had an intrinsic identity. This is why every intrinsic
identity which affirms itself as an objection to the counting-
as-one – that is, as uncounted in the situation in which it
should be counted – comes to light only in the eventual
discovery. It is the eventual discovery which constitutes the
gap between counted for one by the situation, and intrinsic
identity. If we were in a position, from the strict point of
view of the situation itself, to distinguish between what is
counted for one in the situation, and the intrinsic identity
of what is so counted, then this position would not be
immanent to the situation. We would need to be an external
observer, capable of saying: here is an identity, here is what
is counted for one, and we can see that this identity is
outside the count. But since we are always immanent to a
situation, we are necessarily incapable of distinguishing
between what is counted and an intrinsic, uncounted
identity.

What any event reveals – and I think it's particularly
striking in politics – is that there was something which had
its own identity beyond the count, which was not taken
account of. It's why I've always said that an event was, one
way or another, a breakdown of the count. It's also why –
and here we come back to what I was saying about Lacan –
we can equally say, of an event, that it is what demonstrates
what is impossible for the count, as its real, such that the

law of the count is made apparent, as being such that this thing, which wasn't counted, should have been counted.

How would you qualify this fact of always being internal to a situation? Isn't it a kind of transcendental condition, an enabling condition of our existence, that we must always be specific to a situation?

I take it to be an ontological principle, that's the only difference. I've no need to call it transcendental. What ontology tells us, in the theory of the purely multiple, is that, inasmuch as a multiple exists, we can declare its existence only inasmuch as it belongs to another multiple. To exist as a multiple is always to belong to a multiplicity. To exist is to be an element *of*. There is no other possible predicate of existence as such. The immediate consequence is that to exist is to be in a situation, without needing to fall back on the transcendental, since it is a law of being. I try to limit the use of the word 'transcendental' to its Kantian meaning.

'Transcendental' refers back to the subjective conditions of experience, and Kant never stops telling us that it is precisely not a law of being. It is a law of the unity of the phenomenon, not a law of being. If you want to extend the meaning of the word 'transcendental' to the point that you call, in the end, transcendental the first or ultimate condition of thought in general, of existence in general, then at that point I'd agree: yes, it's transcendental.

I know that you are in the middle of reformulating your conception of relationship, and in particular of the relationship between truth and knowledge. How do things stand as of now?

In *L'Etre et l'événement*, I suggest that in every situation there is an encyclopaedia of knowledges, linked to a language of the situation. It's true – and you yourself have raised the objection – that unlike the multiplicity of the situation, which is accounted for in ontology and mathematics, this particular point remains largely ungrounded, or affirmed in an uncritical way. If we assume it, then truth can appear as boring a hole in this encyclopaedia, as subtracting itself from it, or as a diagonal of novelty with respect to it. Both language and knowledge are very important, and they are related, since it is only because there is a language of the situation that there can be predicates, particularities, and thus knowledges.

The reworking I'm engaged in at the moment consists of giving both a legitimacy and a much greater consistency to this double question of the language of the situation and the existence of knowledges. This has naturally led me to rethink the most basic concept of my thinking, which is precisely the notion of situation. In reality, the concept of situation is reduced, in *L'Etre et l'événement*, to the purely multiple, to which is added, slightly from the outside, the language of the situation and its predicates. Setting out from a study of what determines the particularity of a situation, I hope to show that there is necessarily in every situation a predicative universe, which I will call its being-there [*être-là*]. I will try to distinguish the being of the situation, which refers back to ontology, from its being-there – that is, the necessity for every situation to be not simply a being but, coextensive with that being, an appearing [*apparaître*]. It is a doctrine of appearing, but of a non-phenomenal appearing. It's not a matter of an appearing for a subject, but of an appearing as such, as localization. It is a localization that doesn't itself refer back to any particular space or geography but is, rather, an intrinsic localization. It is a supplementary ontological property, in addition to pure multiplicity.

In other words, I'm going to tackle the problem of the distinction between a possible and an effective situation, between possible situation and real situation, since I'll go back over the fact that ontology doesn't settle this question, that it is beneath this point of distinction. Hence the effectivity of a situation, its appearing, can't be deduced from its configuration of multiplicity. There is no transitivity between the one and the other.

At this point, we'll have to ask about the laws of appearing. I think we can maintain the idea that mathematics still explains some of what happens, that we aren't absolutely obliged to leave the realm of the mathematical. Simply, we'll need a slightly new form of mathematicity, one that requires a minimal theory of relation, a *logic*. I call 'logic' a theory of relation as relation, relation between elements, between parts, and so on. I will argue that being-as-being – that is, as beneath the relation between being and being-there – is a pure multiplicity. But I will show how this pure multiplicity is always attached to, distorted by, or reworked by a universe of relations, which will define the logic peculiar to the situation, not merely its being displayed in its multiplicity, or its network of belongings.

This is going to require, on the mathematical side of things, different operators, both logical and topological, and on the philosophical side, an elucidation of the relation between being and being-there. I think I'll be able to draw most of the argument from the relation of order, from the elementary relation of order, order being defined simply as the first dissymmetrical relation – of course, the didactics of the thing, the way of presenting it, is very important to me, and for as long as I haven't fully discovered it, I'm not entirely at ease. I'm going to try to solve the problem – and you can see that I've read your work, and am sensitive to what you've said – by injecting something like dissymmetry into the general edifice, without in any way renouncing it. This means that it will mean something to say that *a* is in relation with *b*, in a relation which is something other than the strict relation of equivalence or equality. I'll take up the relation of order because it is, in the end, mathematically, the most primordial, most abstract, non-symmetrical relation.

My last questions concern the autonomy of truth, its status in relation to the world it exceeds or transcends. What kind of relationship is there, for example, between the truth of a scientific or an artistic discovery and the technical means of its formulation and distribution? What relation is there between an artistic – let's say musical – truth, and the (culturally specific) system of tonality which ensures that the truths of Haydn and Schoenberg – to take examples from your Ethique *– are always truths for certain listeners?*

I think we have to accept that between the effective or real character of any procedure of truth, and the protocol of identification, recognition, designation, or propagation of that truth, there are only individual cases, and no general relationship. We can give very simple examples. Take, for example, Arabo-Andalusian music, which has its own space of development, of creation, of historicity. For a long time it couldn't be identified as such. And then conditions were created in which it became identifiable. It's really an individual case.

This touches on two problems, which I'm currently working on. First problem: does the universalizing identification of a truth have as its condition *sine qua non* something like philosophy? After all, I have myself defended the thesis according to which philosophy does not create truths, but plays a certain role – I didn't say the only role – in their identification and in their compatibility, their compossibility, the evaluation of their time. For me, this is still an open question. Is there always something of the order of philosophy – but how are we to recognize philosophy? – in the universalizing identification of a procedure of truth, regardless of its origin or destination?

This poses the question of the degree of philosophy's own universality. If we admit that philosophy has a capacity – not an exclusive capacity, but one that is proper to it – to identify something as universal, then it's obvious that philosophy has played a major role in the identification of science as such. We know that the identification of art itself, *as art*, as distinct from anything else, is the achievement of philosophy. To generalize: does the identification of procedures of truth always pass through philosophy, necessarily or unnecessarily, or is it a question of situation, of culture? It's an open question, and a fairly complicated one.

The second, still more complicated problem concerns what I call the interconnected juxtaposition [*juxtaposition en réseau*] of truth-procedures. Truth-procedures do not exist as unilaterally unconnected, as entirely independent of each other, each following their own path. They are constituted in a network, they cross each other. Part of the problem is a matter of knowing, for example, the points of connection between scientific procedure, its successive breaks, its discoveries, and the rules of political protocol. It's a very real question. You yourself have said that there is in science something which is hidden beneath machinery or equipment that is not entirely its own, but which nevertheless largely contains it. In the same way, I've always been fascinated by the network of relations between love and art. We know very well that there is something within the development of love itself which is certainly marked, signed [*signé*] from within, by the novel, by the whole history of this question and the way it's been handled artistically, over successive strata. To such an extent that where the artistic situation is quite obviously different – I'm thinking of China, for example – I've often thought that love itself must be different. These are questions of interconnection [*réseau*]; the truth-procedures resonate with each other, in their connections and crossings.

So far I've been very analytical in working on this question, very Cartesian. I've separated the procedures from each other, examined their type, their numericity, and so forth, but I'm perfectly aware that in a situation [*en situation*], in the realm of singularity, this is not exactly how things look. There are always several procedures working through entangled or interconnected situations. It's what I hope to explain, once I've deciphered and symbolized the problem, probably according to my own concept of culture. In the end, a culture, to the extent that it can be thought or identified by philosophy, is a singular interconnected configuration of truth-procedures.

I think there are truth-procedures everywhere, and that they are always universal; that a Chinese novel, Arabic algebra, Iranian music ... that all this is, in the end, universal by right. Simply, the conditions of their concrete universalization have followed a complicated history. On the other hand, I would admit that there is an element of the cultural site, which I would see in a system of interconnection, in which there is always something contingent, and also an aspect of sedimentation, of conservation, which is irreducibly particular. Here I'm speaking prospectively, slightly feeling my way forward, but I hope to be able to say how I conceive of a culture, in something other than empirical fashion. I'm perfectly aware that there are cultural universes, linguistic universes. But I'd like to be able to cross through this empirical reality in a slightly different way.

Just what is culturally specific here? How do we measure the immanent universality of an artistic truth, to limit the question only to that? Can it really be anything other than, on the one hand, a kind of pure or living (and therefore ephemeral) creativity – such that Schoenberg's truth, say, persisted or will persist as long as it continues to inspire new creations that remain faithful in some way to this inspiration? Or, on the other hand, a variant of the assertion of its own universal truth? This would limit literary truth, for instance, to the confines of what Bourdieu describes as the 'literary field' – the field established by the proclamation, from Flaubert through Mallarmé, Blanchot and beyond, of an intransitive literary sovereignty, a word purified of worldly knowledge and communication.[13] Most of your poetic examples seem to conform to this idea.

No doubt it's only because I am of this era. Perhaps my own taste, my own site, my own set of interconnections [réseau], have been drawn mainly from this. But I certainly wouldn't make of it a universal maxim. I don't at all think that the affirmation of sovereignty is essential to an artistic configuration. I try to name artistic sequences not so much with proper names, nor through the regime of works of art, but through what I call configurations. In Rosen's book on Haydn, Mozart and Beethoven, what is revealed is a configuration, which he calls the classical style.[14] Obviously, most of my preferred poetic examples – I'm perfectly aware of it – belong to such a configuration.

Paris, 17 November 1997

Notes

1. First published in *Angelaki* 3:3 (1998), 113–33. All footnotes in the interview were written by the interviewer.
2. *La Distance politique* 22 (June 1997): 3. Both terms, *sans-papiers* and *foyers ouvriers*, are difficult to translate without shifting the frame of cultural reference entirely. The long government campaign against the mostly West African and Algerian *sans-papiers* is comparable in its intensity to that waged in the United States against mostly Latin American 'illegal immigrants'. Badiou's militant commitment to the full naturalization of all immigrants living and working in France dates back more than twenty years.

   Foyers ouvriers are collective residences, mainly occupied by single working men (or men whose families remain in their country of origin); often made up of inhabitants from the same place of origin, they are generally marked by a high degree of social cohesion and mutual support. In the last couple of years, the *foyers* in certain Paris suburbs have come under attack from reformist mayors; several have been destroyed. Badiou and L'Organisation Politique which he co-founded in 1984–85 have been instrumental in promoting the campaign for their protection and reconstruction.

3. The term connotes something like the expression 'the New World Order', that is, the ubiquitous, 'pragmatic' free-market liberalism that has become the very form of contemporary *necessity.*

4. In the summer of 1996, hundreds of African immigrants occupied the Saint Bernard church for several months, in a direct refutation of their official characterization as '*clandestins*'. After being expelled from the church by force in August 1996, and again evicted from the town hall of the 18th *arrondissement* in Paris in June 1997, the Saint Bernard campaign has organized – with the Organisation Politique, among other groups – a series of major Paris rallies (15 and 22 November 1997, 6 December 1997, and February 7 1998 . . .). Throughout this campaign, the emphasis has been on the militant *subjective presence* of the *sans-papiers* – that they are not somehow 'alien' or 'invisible', but simply *here* as ordinary workers under extraordinary pressure. 'Saint Bernard is proof of a strong principle of auto-constitution, in the sense that people decided one day to come out from their homes and to constitute themselves collectively in their demand for residence papers' (*La Distance politique*, 19–20 (April 1997), 7). Such directly political or subjective mobilization has nothing to do with the pious valorization of certain people as 'disadvantaged' or *exclus.*

5. *La Distance politique* 25 (November 1997), 3. *La Distance politique* is the journal of the Organisation Politique, a relatively short bulletin (usually between 4 and 15 pages), published on average four times a year, printing articles and editorials detailing particular demonstrations and rallies, interviews with workers or immigrant groups, discussions of electoral campaigns and results, and general reflections on 'what is to

be done'. The first three issues of *La Distance politique* included brief analyses of canonical works by Marx, Lenin and Mao, in that order; issue 5 carried an article on Althusser. Since then the emphasis has been almost exclusively practical, and *La Distance politique* has remained much more of an organizing tool than any sort of contribution to 'political theory'.

In keeping with Badiou's understanding of a political *subject*, the Organisation Politique adheres to a strict form of collective responsibility, and as a rule the positions expressed by *La Distance politique* can be taken as fully consistent with Badiou's own. Badiou has always treated the Organisation Politique as nothing less than a 'subjective condition of my philosophy' (Alain Badiou, *Abrégé de métapolitique*, 117).

6. L'Organisation Politique, *Cahier No. 4, Ni statut spécial, ni intégration: On est tous ici, on est tous d'ici* (May 1997), 4.

7. L'Organisation Politique, *Cahier No. 4*, 3.

8. Alain Badiou, *Saint Paul ou la fondation de l'universalisme*, 106.

9. See Karl Marx and Friedrich Engels, *The Communist Manifesto*, 82.

10. Hannah Arendt, *On Revolution*, 206.

11. 'It's entirely possible that there was no event at all. I really don't know' (Alain Badiou, 'Being by Numbers', *Artforum* 33:2 (October 1994), 123).

12. Alain Badiou, *L'Ethique*, 52/58–9.

13. Pierre Bourdieu, *Les Règles de l'art: Structure et génèse du champ littéraire*, 1992 [1996].

14. Charles Rosen, *The Classical Style: Haydn, Mozart, Beethoven*, 1976.

Bibliography

Works cited in *Ethics*

Alleg, Henri, *La Question*. Paris: Minuit, 1958.

Aristotle, *The Nicomachean Ethics*, trans. David Ross, revised by J. L. Ackrill and J. O. Urmson. Oxford: Oxford University Press, 1980.

Cohen, Paul J., *Set Theory and the Continuum Hypothesis*. New York: W. A. Benjamin, 1966.

Diogenes Laertius, *Lives of Eminent Philosophers*, with an English translation by R. D. Hicks [2 vols]. London: Heinemann, 1925.

Farias, Victor, *Heidegger et le nazisme*. Paris: Verdier, 1985. Translated by Paul Burrell and Gabriel R. Ricci with Dominic Di Bernardi as *Heidegger and Nazism*. Philadelphia, PA: Temple University Press, 1989.

Glucksmann, André, *Les maîtres penseurs*. Paris: Grasset, 1977. Translated by Brian Pearce as *The Master Thinkers*. Brighton: Harvester Press, 1980.

Gödel, Kurt, *Collected Works*, ed. Soloman Feferman. 2 vols. Oxford: Oxford University Press, 1986.

Habermas, Jürgen, *The Theory of Communicative Action*, trans.

Thomas McCarthy. 2 vols. Boston, MA: Beacon Press, 1983–85.

Hegel, Georg Wilhelm Friedrich, *The Phenomenology of Spirit*, trans. A. V. Miller. Oxford: Clarendon Press, 1977.

Kant, Immanuel, *Groundwork of the Metaphysics of Morals*, trans. Mary Gregor. Cambridge: Cambridge University Press, 1997.

Lacan, Jacques, *Ecrits*. Paris: Seuil, 1966. Partially translated by Alan Sheridan as *Ecrits: A Selection*. London: Tavistock, 1977.

Lacoue-Labarthe, Philippe, *La fiction du politique: Heidegger, l'art et la politique*. Paris: Christian Bougois, 1987. Translated by Chris Turner as *Heidegger, Art and Politics: The Fiction of the Political*. Oxford: Blackwell, 1990.

Lacoue-Labarthe, Philippe, and Nancy, Jean-Luc, *L'absolu littéraire: théorie de la littérature du romantisme allemand*. Paris: Seuil, 1978. Translated by Philip Barnard and Cheryl Lester as *The Literary Absolute: The Theory of Literature in German Romanticism*. Albany: State University of New York Press, 1988.

Lévinas, Emmanuel, *Totalité et infini*. The Hague: Martinus Nijhoff, 1961 (Livre de poche edn.). Translated by Alphonso Lingis as *Totality and Infinity*. Pittsburgh, PA: Duquesne University Press, 1969.

Nietzsche, Friedrich, *The Genealogy of Morals*, trans. Douglas Smith. Oxford: Oxford University Press, 1996.

Plato, *The Collected Dialogues*, ed. Edith Hamilton and Huntington Cairns. Princeton, NJ: Princeton University Press, 1961.

Shalamov, Varlam Tikhonovich, *Kolyma Tales*, trans. John Glad. New York: W.W. Norton, 1980.

Spinoza, Baruch, *Ethics*, trans. Samuel Shirley. Indianapolis, IN: Hackett, 1992.

Winter, Cécile, *Qu'en est-il de l'historicité actuelle de la clinique?* [unpublished dissertation].

Other works cited

Arendt, Hannah, *On Revolution* [1963]. Harmondsworth: Penguin, 1990.

Beckett, Samuel, *L'Innommable*. Paris: Minuit, 1953.

Barwise, John, ed., *Handbook of Mathematical Logic*. Amsterdam: North Holland, 1977.

Bourdieu, Pierre, *Les règles de l'art: Genèse et structure du champ littéraire*. Paris: Seuil, 1992. Translated by Susan Emanuel. Stanford, CA: Stanford University Press, 1996.

Deleuze, Gilles, *Logique du sens*. Paris: Minuit, 1969. Translated by Mark Lester with Charles Stivale as *The Logic of Sense*. New York: Columbia University Press, 1990.

Derrida, Jacques, *De la grammatologie*. Paris: Minuit, 1967. Translated by Gayatri Chakravorty Spivak as *Of Grammatology* [1976]. Baltimore, MD: Johns Hopkins University Press, 1998.

——*L'Ecriture et la différence*. Paris: Seuil, 1967. Translated by Alan Bass as *Writing and Difference*. Chicago: University of Chicago Press, 1978.

——*Donner le temps*. Paris: Galilée, 1991. Translated by Peggy Kamuf as *Given Time. 1. Counterfeit Money*. Chicago: University of Chicago Press, 1992.

——*Donner la mort*, in Jean-Michel Rabaté and Michael Wetzel, eds, *L'Ethique du don, Jacques Derrida et la pensée du don*. Paris: Transition, 1992. Translated by Davil Wills as

The Gift of Death. Chicago: University of Chicago Press, 1995.

——*Points de suspension. Entretiens*. Paris: Galilée, 1994.

——*Adieu à Emmanuel Lévinas*. Paris: Galilée, 1997.

——'Intellectual Courage: An Interview' [1998], http://culturemachine.tees.ac.uk/frm_fl.htm. French version: http://www.hydra.umn.edu/derrida/zeit.html.

——*Sur Parole*. Paris: Editions de l'Aube, 1999.

Heidegger, Martin, *Basic Writings*, ed. David Farrell Krell. London: HarperCollins, 1993.

Irigaray, Luce, *Speculum de l'autre femme*. Paris: Minuit, 1974. Translated by Gillian C. Gill as *Speculum of the Other Woman*. Ithaca, NY: Cornell University Press, 1985.

——*Ce sexe qui n'est pas un*. Paris: Minuit, 1977. Translated by Catherine Porter with Carolyn Burke as *This Sex Which Is Not One*. Ithaca, NY: Cornell University Press, 1985.

——*Ethique de la différence sexuelle*. Paris: Minuit, 1984. Translated by Carolyn Burke and Gillian C. Gill as *An Ethics of Sexual Difference*. London: Athlone Press, 1993.

——*Sexes et parentés*. Paris: Minuit, 1987. Translated by Gillian C. Gill as *Sexes and Genealogies*. New York: Columbia University Press, 1993.

——*Le Temps de la différence: Pour une révolution pacifique*. Paris: Librairie générale française, 1989. Translated by Karin Montin as *Thinking the Difference: For a Peaceful Revolution*. London: Athlone Press, 1994.

——*Je, Tu, Nous. Pour une culture de la différence*. Paris: Grasset, 1990. Translated by Alison Martin as *Je, Tu, Nous: Toward a Culture of Difference*. London: Routledge, 1993.

——*Irigaray Reader*, ed. Margaret Whitford. Oxford: Blackwells, 1991.

——*J'aime à toi. Esquisse d'une félicité dans l'histoire*. Paris:

Grasset, 1992. Translated by Alison Martin as *I Love to You: Sketch for a Felicity Within History*. London: Routledge, 1994.

——*et al.*, *Sexes et genres à travers les langues: éléments de communication sexuelle*. Paris: Grasset, 1990.

Kant, Immanuel, *Critique of Pure Reason*, trans. Werner S. Pluhar. Indianapolis, IN: Hackett, 1996. (The pagination to this and all other references to Kant's works is, as is customary, to the standard German edition.)

——*Critique of Practical Reason*, trans. Mary Gregor. Cambridge: Cambridge University Press, 1997.

Lacan, Jacques, *Ecrits*. Paris: Seuil, 1966; partially trans. Alan Sheridan. London: Tavistock, 1977.

——*Le Séminaire I*. ed. Jacques-Alain Miller. Paris: Seuil, 1975; trans. John Forrester. New York: Norton, 1988.

——*Le Séminaire II*, ed. Jacques-Alain Miller. Paris: Seuil, 1978; trans. Sylvana Tomaselli. New York: Norton, 1988.

——*Le Séminaire III*, ed. Jacques-Alain Miller. Paris: Seuil, 1981; trans. Russell Grigg. London: Routledge, 1988.

——*Le Séminaire VII*, ed. Jacques-Alain Miller. Paris: Seuil, 1986; trans. Denis Porter. London: Routledge, 1988.

——*Le Séminaire XI*, ed. Jacques-Alain Miller. Paris: Seuil, 1973; trans. Alan Sheridan. NY: Norton, 1988.

——*Le Séminaire XX*, ed. Jacques-Alain Miller. Paris: Seuil, 1975.

Lévinas, Emmanuel, *Autrement qu'être ou au-delà de l'essence*. The Hague: Martinus Nijhoff, 1974 (Livre de poche edn). Translated by Alphonso Lingis as *Otherwise than Being or Beyond Essence*. The Hague: Martinus Nijhoff, 1981.

——*Basic Philosophical Writings*, ed. Adriaan T. Peperzak, Simon Critchley and Robert Bernasconi. Bloomington: University of Indiana Press, 1996.

Marx, Karl, and Engels, Friedrich, *The Communist Manifesto*, trans. Samuel Moore. Harmondsworth: Penguin, 1967.

Pascal, Blaise, *Oeuvres complètes*. Paris: Gallimard, Pléiade, 1954.

Rosen, Charles, *The Classical Style: Haydn, Mozart, Beethoven* [1976]. New York: Norton, 1997.

Spivak, Gayatri Chakravorty, 'What Is It For': Functions of Postcolonial Criticism', *Nineteenth Century Contexts* 18 (1992), 1–8.

——*Outside in the Teaching Machine*. London: Routledge, 1993.

——'In the New World Order', in Antonio Callari *et al.*, eds, *Marxism in the Postmodern Age*. New York: Guilford Press, 1994. 89–97.

——'Love, Cruelty and Cultural Talks in the Hot Peace', *Parallax* 1 (September 1995), 1–31.

——*The Spivak Reader*, ed. Donna Landry and Gerald Maclean. London: Routledge, 1996.

——'Diasporas Old and New: Women in a Transnational World', *Textual Practices* 10:2 (1996), 245–69.

——*The Critique of Postcolonial Reason: Toward a History of the Vanishing Present*. Cambridge, MA: Harvard University Press, 1999.

Žižek, Slavoj, *Tarrying with the Negative: Kant, Hegel, and the Critique of Ideology*. Durham, NC: Duke University Press, 1993.

——*The Metastases of Enjoyment: Six Essays on Woman and Causality*. London and New York: Verso, 1994.

——*The Plague of Fantasies*. London and New York: Verso, 1997.

——*The Ticklish Subject: The Absent Centre of Political Ontology*. London and New York: Verso, 1999.

Zupančič, Alenka, *Ethics of the Real: Kant, Lacan.* London and New York: Verso, 2000.

Works by Alain Badiou

Books of philosophy, politics and criticism

Le Concept de modèle. Introduction à une épistémologie matérialiste des mathématiques. Paris: Maspero, 1972.

Théorie de la contradiction. Paris: Maspero, 1975.

De l'idéologie. Paris: Maspero, 1976.

Théorie du sujet. Paris: Seuil, 1982.

Peut-on penser la politique? Paris: Seuil, 1985.

L'Etre et l'événement. Paris: Seuil, 1988. Translation in progress by Oliver Feltham, as *Being and Event.* Probable publication details: London, Athlone Press, 2003. The two chapters on 'Hegel' and 'Descartes/Lacan' were translated by Marcus Coelen and Sam Gillespie and Sigi Jöttkandt with Daniel Collins respectively in the first volume of *Umbr(a)* 1 (Buffalo, NY: SUNY, 1996).

Manifeste pour la philosophie. Paris: Seuil, 1989. Translated by Norman Madarasz as *Manifesto for Philosophy.* Albany, NY: SUNY, 1999.

Le Nombre et les nombres. Paris: Seuil, 1990.

Rhapsodie pour le théâtre. Paris: Le Spectateur français, 1990.

D'un désastre obscur (Droit, Etat, Politique). Paris: L'Aube, 1991.

Conditions. Paris: Seuil, 1992. Two chapters ('The (Re)turn of Philosophy *Itself* and 'Definition of Philosophy' are included in Madarasz's translation of the *Manifesto for Philosophy* (Albany, NY: SUNY, 1999). Two other chapters ('Psychoanalysis and Philosophy' and 'What is Love?') appeared in *Umbr(a)* 1 (Buffalo, NY: SUNY, 1996).

Beckett: L'incrévable désir. Paris: Hachette, 1995.

Gilles Deleuze: 'La clameur de l'Etre.' Paris: Hachette, 1997. Translated by Louise Burchill as *Gilles Deleuze: The Clamor of Being.* Minneapolis: University of Minnesota Press, 2000.

Saint Paul et la fondation de l'universalisme. Paris: PUF, 1997.

Court traité d'ontologie transitoire. Paris: Seuil, 1998.

Abrégé de métapolitique. Paris: Seuil, 1998.

Petit manuel d'inesthétique. Paris: Seuil, 1998.

Le Siècle. Paris: Seuil, 2001 [bilingual edition: English translation by Alberto Toscano].

Novels and plays

Almagestes [novel]. Paris: Seuil, 1964.

Portulans [novel]. Paris: Seuil, 1967.

L'Echarpe rouge [romanopéra]. Paris: Maspero, 1979.

Ahmed le subtil [theatre]. Arles: Actes Sud, 1994.

Ahmed se fâche, suivi par Ahmed philosophe [theatre]. Arles, Actes Sud, 1995.

Citrouilles [theatre]. Arles, Actes Sud, 1995.

Calme bloc ici-bas [novel]. Paris: P.O.L., 1997.

Articles, pamphlets and interviews

'L'autonomie du processus historique.' *Cahiers Marxistes–Léninistes* (Paris: Ecole Normale Supérieure) 12–13 (1966): 77–89.

'L'Autorisation' [short story]. *Les Temps Modernes* 258 (1967): 761–89.

'Le (re)commencement du matérialisme dialectique.' Review of Althusser, *Pour Marx* and Althusser *et al.*, *Lire le Capital. Critique* 240 (May 1967): 438–67.

'La subversion infinitésimale.' *Cahiers pour l'analyse* (Paris: Ecole Normale Supérieure) 9 (1968): 118–37.

7'Marque et manque: à propos du zéro.' *Cahiers pour l'analyse* 10 (1969): 150–73.

Badiou *et al.*, *Contribution au problème de la construction d'un parti marxiste–léniniste de type nouveau*. Paris: Maspero, 1969.

Le mouvement ouvrier révolutionnaire contre le syndicalisme [pamphlet]. Marseille: Potemkine, 1976.

Badiou and Sylvain Lazarus, eds, *La Situation actuelle sur le front de la philosophie*, Cahiers Yenan No. 4. Paris: Maspero, 1977.

'Le Flux et le parti (dans les marges de *L'Anti-Œdipe*)', in *La Situation actuelle sur le front de la philosophie* . . . (1977). 24–41.

La 'contestation' dans le P.C.F. [pamphlet]. Marseille: Potemkine, 1978.

Le Noyau rationnel de la dialectique [collective work]. Paris: Maspero, 1978.

Jean-Paul Sartre [pamphlet]. Paris: Potemkine, 1981.

'Poème mise à mort suivi de "L'ombre où s'y claire"', in *Le vivant et l'artificiel*. Sgraffite: Festival d'Avignon, 1984. 19–23.

'Custos, quid noctis?' Review of Lyotard, *Le Différend*. *Critique* 450 (November 1984): 851–63.

'Six propriétés de la vérité.' *Ornicar?* 32 (January 1985): 39–67; continued in *Ornicar?* 33 (April 1985): 120–49.

'Les noeuds du théâtre,' *L'Art du théâtre* 7 (1987): 83–8 [reprinted in *Rhapsodie pour le théâtre*].

'L'état théâtral en son Etat,' *L'Art du théâtre* 8 (1988): 11–28 [reprinted in *Rhapsodie pour le théâtre*].

Badiou *et al.*, *Une soirée philosophique* [pamphlet]. Paris: Potemkine/Seuil, 1988.

'D'un sujet enfin sans objet.' *Cahiers Confrontations* 20 (1989): 13–22. Translated by Bruce Fink as 'On a Finally Objectless Subject', in Eduardo Cadava, Peter Connor and Jean-Luc Nancy, eds, *Who Comes After the Subject?* London: Routledge, 1991. 24–32.

'Untitled Response.' In *Témoigner du différend. Quand phraser ne peut. Autour de Jean-François Lyotard*, ed. Francis Guibal and Jacob Rogozînskî. Paris: Osiris, 1989. 109–13.

'Dix-neuf réponses à beaucoup plus d'objections.' *Cahiers du Collège Internationale de philosophie* 8 (1989): 247–68.

Samuel Beckett: L'Ecriture du générique [pamphlet]. Paris: Editions du Perroquet, 1989. 35 pp. Partial English translation by Alban Urbanas, in *Journal of Beckett Studies* 4:1 (1994): 13–21.

'L'Entretien de Bruxelles.' *Les Temps modernes*, No. 526 (1990): 1–26.

'Pourquoi Antoine Vitez a-t-il abandonné Chaillot pour le Français?' *L'Art du théâtre* 10 (1990): 143–5.

Review of Gilles Deleuze, *Le Pli: Leibniz et le baroque. Annuaire philosophique 1988–1989*. Paris: Seuil, 1990. 161–84. English translation by Thelma Sowley in Constantin Boundas and Dorothea Olkowski, eds, *Gilles Deleuze: The Theatre of Philosophy*. New York: Columbia University Press, 1994. 51–69.

'Saisissement, dessaisie, fidélité' [on Sartre]. *Les Temps Modernes*, 531–3, vol. 1 (1990): 14–22.

'Ta faute, ô graphie!' In *Pour la photographie III*. Paris: Germs, 1990. 261–5.

'Objectivité et objectalité [1991]. Review of Monique David-Ménard, *La folie dans la raison pure: Kant lecteur de Swedenborg*. Paris: Vrin, 1990. Unpublished typescript, 11 pp.

'L'Etre, l'événement et la militance.' Interview with Nicole-Edith Thévenin. *Futur antérieur* 8 (1991): 13–23.

Monde contemporain et désir de philosophie [pamphlet]. Reims: Cahier de Noria, No. 1, 1992.

Casser en deux l'histoire du monde? [pamphlet]. Paris: Le Perroquet, 1992.

'Y-a-t-il une théorie du sujet chez George Canguilhem?' In *Georges Canguilhem, Philosophe, historien des sciences.* Bibliothèque du Collège International de la Philosophie. Paris: Albin Michel, 1992. 295–304. Translated by Graham Burchell as 'Is there a theory of the subject in Georges Canguilhem?' *Economy and Society* 27:2/3 (1998): 225–33.

'Le pays comme principe.' *Le Monde. Bilan économique et social 1992*: 134–5.

'Les lieux de la vérité.' Interview with Jacques Henri. *Art Press spécial: '20 ans: l'histoire continue'*, hors série no. 13 (1992): 113–18.

'L'Age des poètes.' In *La Politique des poètes. Pourquoi des poètes en temps de détresse*, ed. Jacques Rancière. Paris: Albin Michel, 1992. 21–38.

'Le statut philosophique du poème après Heidegger.' In *Penser après Heidegger*, ed. Jacques Poulain and Wolfgang Schirmacher. Paris: L'Harmattan, 1992. 263–8.

'Réponses écrites d'Alain Badiou.' Interview with student group at the University of Paris VIII (Vincennes/Saint-Denis). *Philosophie, philosophie* 4 (1992): 66–71.

'Qu'est-ce que Louis Althusser entend par "philosophie"?' In *Politique et philosophie dans l'oeuvre de Louis Althusser*, ed. Sylvain Lazarus. Paris: PUF, 1993. 29–45.

'Que pense le poème?' In *L'art est-il une connaissance?*, ed. Roger Pol Droit. Paris: Le Monde Editions, 1993. 214–24.

'Nous pouvons redéployer la philosophie.' Interview with Roger Pol Droit. Le Monde, 31 August 1993, p. 2.

'Sur le livre de Françoise Proust, *Le ton de l'histoire.'* Les Temps Modernes 565/566 (1993): 238–48.

Topos, ou Logiques de l'onto-logique. Une introduction pour philosophes, tome 1. Unpublished, 1993. 153 pp.

'1977, une formidable regression intellectuelle'. *Le Monde 1944/1994*, November 1994.

'Art et philosophie.' In *Artistes et philosophes: éducateurs?*, ed. Christian Descamps. Paris: Centre Georges Pompidou, 1994. 155–70.

'Being by Numbers.' Interview with Lauren Sedofsky. *Artforum* 33.2 (October 1994): 84–7, 118, 123–4.

'Silence, solipsisme, sainteté: l'antiphilosophie de Wittgenstein.' *BARCA! Poésie, Politique, Psychanalyse* 3 (1994): 13–53.

'L'Etre du nombre' [1994]. Unpublished typescript (partially published in *Court traité*), 15 pp.

'La Question de l'être aujourd'hui' [1994]. Unpublished lectures (partially published in *Court traité*) given at the Ecole Normale Supérieure, Paris.

'Qu'est-ce qu'un thermidorien?' In *La République et la terreur*, ed. Catherine Kintzler and Hadi Rizk. Paris: Kimé, 1995. 53–64 [reprinted in *Abrégé de métapolitique*].

'Platon et/ou Aristote–Leibniz. Théorie des ensembles et théorie des Topos sous l'oeil du philosophe.' In *L'Objectivité mathématique. Platonismes et structures formelles*, ed. Marco Panza. Paris: Masson, 1995. 61–83 (partially published in *Court traité*).

'L'Impératif de la négation' [1995]. Review of Guy Lardreau, *La Véracité* (Paris: Verdier, 1993). Unpublished typescript, 14 pp.

'Ethique et psychiatrie' [1995]. Unpublished typescript, 13 pp.

'Préface.' In Henry Bauchau, *Heureux les délirants: poèmes 1950–1995*. Brussels: Labor, 1995. 10 pp.

'Pour un tombeau. Deleuze, hommage au philosophe disparu. Qu'est-ce que penser?' *Le Monde*, 10 November 1995.

'Jean Borreil: le style d'une pensée.' In *Jean Borreil: la raison de l'autre*, ed. Maurice Matieu and Patrice Vermeren. Paris: L'Harmattan, 1996. 29–35.

'Les gestes de la pensée [on François Châtelet].' *Les Temps Modernes* 586 (1996): 196–204.

'Penser la singularité: les noms innommables.' Review of Sylvain Lazarus, *Anthropologie du nom* [1996]. *Critique* 595 (December 1996): 1074–95 [reprinted in *Abrégé de métapolitique*].

'Logologie contre ontologie.' Review of Barbara Cassin, *L'Effet sophistique* [1995]. *Po&sie* 78 (December 1996): 111–16.

'Vérités et justice,' ed. Jacques Poulain, *Qu'est-ce que la justice? Devant l'autel de l'histoire*. Paris: Presses Universitaires de Vincennes, December 1996. 275–81.

'Lieu et déclaration.' In *Paroles à la bouche du présent*, ed. Natacha Michel. Marseille: Al Dante, 1997. 177–84.

'L'insoumission de Jeanne.' *Esprit* 238 (December 1997): 26–33.

[with Sylvain Lazarus and Natacha Michel], 'Une France pour tous.' *Le Monde*, 9 December 1997.

'Le plus-de-Voir' [on Godard's *Histoire(s) du cinéma*, 1998]. *Artpress*, hors série 1998, 5pp.

'Ce qui arrive' [on Beckett, 1997–98]. Unpublished typescript, 4 pp.

'Politics and Philosophy.' Interview with Peter Hallward. *Angelaki*, 3:3 (1998): 113–33. Reprinted in this volume.

'Penser le surgissement de l'événement'. Interview with E. Burdeau and F. Ramone, *Cahiers du Cinéma*, numéro spécial (May 1998): 9 pp.

'Paul le saint.' Interview with J. Henric. *Artpress* 235 (May 1998): 3 pp.

'On ne passe pas' [on Badiou's own practice of writing]. *Théorie, littérature, enseignement* (Revue du Département de Lettres, Université de Paris VIII) 16 (Autumn 1998): 17–20.

'Huit thèses sur l'universel.' Unpublished lecture, part of the *Forum sur l'universel* (with Etienne Balibar and Monique David-Ménard) held at the Collège International de Philosophie, Paris, 4 November 1998 (tapescript available at the Collège).

'Théâtre et politique dans la comédie.' *Où va le théâtre?* Hoëbeke, 1999. 8 pp.

'La Scène du Deux,' in Badiou *et al.*, sous la direction de L'Ecole de la Cause Freudienne. *De l'amour*. Paris: Flammarion, 'Champs' 1999. 14 pp.

'Entretien avec Alain Badiou.' Interview with N. Poirier. *Le philosophoire* 9 (1999): 14–32.

'Considérations sur l'état actuel du cinéma, et sur les moyens de penser cet état sans avoir à conclure que le cinéma est mort ou mourant.' *L'Art du cinéma* 24 (March 1999): 7–22.

'La Sainte-Alliance et ses serviteurs' [on Kosovo]. *Le Monde*, 20 May 1999 (available at: http://www.lemonde.fr/article/0,2320,6246,00.html).

'De la langue française comme évidement' [1999]. Unpublished typescript, 9 pp.

'Les langues de Wittgenstein.' *Rue Descartes* 26 (December 1999: 107–16.

'Entretien avec Alain Badiou' [1999]. Unpublished typescript, 6 pp.

'Théorie axiomatique du sujet. Notes du cours 1996–1998.'
Unpublished typescript, 121 pp.

'Les lieux de la philosophie,' *Bleue: Littératures en force* 1
(Winter 2000): 120–25.

'L'Existence et la mort,' in Christian Delacampagne and
Robert Maggiori, eds, *Philosopher T2* Paris: Fayard, 2000.
10 pp.

'Metaphysics and the Critique of Metaphysics,' trans.
Alberto Toscano, *Pli* (*Warwick Journal of Philosophy*) 10
(2000): 174–90.

'Of Life as a Name of Being, or Deleuze's Vitalist Ontology'
[translation of *Court traité d'ontologie transitoire*, ch. 4],
trans. Alberto Toscano, *Pli* (*Warwick Journal of Philosophy*)
10 (2000): 191–9.

'Psychoanalysis and Philosophy,' trans. Oliver Feltham.
Analysis 9 (Melbourne, 2000): 1–8.

'L'Etre-là: mathématique du transcendental' [2000]. Unpublished typescript, 109 pp.

'Un, Multiple, Multiplicité(s)' [response to critics of Badiou's
Deleuze, 1997]. *Multitudes* 1 (March 2000): 195–211.

'Saint Paul, fondateur du sujet universel,' *Etudes Théologiques
et Religieuses* 75 (March 2000): 323–33.

'Une tâche philosophique: être contemporain de Pessoa.' In
Colloque de Cerisy: Pessoa, ed. Pascal Dethurens and Maria-
Alzira Seixo. Paris: Christian Bougois, 2000. 141–55.

'L'Arrogance impériale dans ses oeuvres'. *Le Monde*, 25
March 2000.

'Vide, séries, clairière. Essai sur la prose de Severo Sarduy'
[on Sarduy's novel *Colibri* (1984)], in Severo Sarduy, *Obras
completas*, ed. François Wahl. 2000.

Works on Alain Badiou

Alliez, Eric, 'Badiou/Deleuze', *Futur antérieur* 43 (1998): 49–54.

——'Que la vérité soit', in Eric Alliez, *De l'impossibilité de la phénoménologie: Sur la philosophie française contemporaine*. Paris: Vrin, 1995. 81–7.

Brassier, Ray, 'Stellar Void or Cosmic Animal? Badiou and Deleuze', *PLI (Warwick Journal of Philosophy)* 10 (2000): 200–17.

Burchill, Louise, 'Translator's Preface: Portraiture in Philosophy, or Shifting Perspective', in Badiou, *Deleuze: The Clamor of Being*. Minneapolis: University of Minnesota Press, 2000. vii–xxiii.

Châtelet, Gilles, Review of *Le Nombre et les Nombres. Annuaire philosophique 1989–1990*. Paris: Seuil, 1991. 117–33.

Critchley, Simon, 'Demanding Approval: On the Ethics of Alain Badiou', *Radical Philosophy* 100 (2000): 16–27.

Desanti, Jean-Toussaint, 'Quelques remarques à propos de l'ontologie intrinsèque d'Alain Badiou', *Temps modernes* 526 (May 1990): 61–71.

Fink, Bruce, 'Alain Badiou', *Umbr(a)* 1 (Buffalo: SUNY, 1996): 11–12.

Gil, José, 'Quatre méchantes notes sur un livre méchant.' Review of Badiou, *Deleuze. Futur antérieur* 43 (1998): 71–84.

Gillespie, Sam, 'Hegel Unsutured (An Addendum to Badiou)', *Umbr(a)* 1 (Buffalo: SUNY, 1996): 57–69.

Hallward, Peter, 'Generic Sovereignty: The Philosophy of Alain Badiou', *Angelaki* 3:3 (1998), 87–111.

——'Ethics without Others: A Reply to Simon Critchley', *Radical Philosophy* 102 (July 2000), 27–31.

———*Subject to Truth: An Introduction to the Philosophy of Alain Badiou*. Minneapolis: University of Minnesota Press, 2001.

Jambet, Christian, 'Alain Badiou: *L'Etre et l'événement*', *Annuaire philosophique 1987–1988*. Paris: Seuil, 1989. 141–83.

Kouvélakis, Eustache, 'La politique dans ses limites.' Unpublished paper given at the Maison française, Oxford, 2 March 2000.

Lacoue-Labarthe, Philippe, Untitled Discussion of *L'Etre et l'événement*, *Cahiers du Collège International de philosophie* 8 (1989): 201–10.

———'Poésie, philosophie, politique.' In *La Politique des poètes. Pourquoi des poètes en temps de détresse*, ed. Jacques Rancière. Paris: Albin Michel, 1992. 39–63.

Lecercle, Jean-Jacques, 'Cantor, Lacan, Mao, Beckett, *même combat*: The Philosophy of Alain Badiou', *Radical Philosophy* 93 (January 1999): 6–13.

Lyotard, Jean-François, Untitled Discussion of *L'Etre et L'événement*. *Cahiers du Collège International de philosophie* 8 (1989): 227–46.

Madarasz, Norman, 'Translator's Introduction', in Badiou, *Manifesto for Philosophy*. Albany, NY: SUNY, 1999.

Pesson, René, Review of *Manifeste pour la philosophie. Annuaire philosophique* 1988–89. Paris: Seuil, 1989. 243–51.

Ramond, Charles, ed., *Alain Badiou: 'La pensée forte'* [papers given at the international conference on Badiou's work at Bordeaux, 21–23 October, 1999]. Forthcoming.

Rancière, Jacques, Untitled Discussion of *L'Etre et l'événement*. *Cahiers du Collège International de philosophie* 8 (1989): 211–26.

Sichère, Bernard, 'Badiou lit Deleuze', *Critique* 605 (October 1997), 722ff.

Simont, Juliette, 'Le pur et l'impur (sur deux questions de

l'histoire de la philosophie dans *L'Etre et l'événement).'* *Temps modernes* 526 (May 1990): 27–60.

Terray, Emmanuel, 'La politique dans *L'Etre et l'événement.'* *Temps modernes* 526 (May 1990): 72–8.

Toscano, Alberto, 'To Have Done with the End of Philosophy.' Review of Badiou's *Manifesto* and *Deleuze. Pli (Warwick Journal of Philosophy)* 9 (2000): 220–39.

Verstraeten, Pierre, 'Philosophies de l'événement: Badiou et quelques autres.' *Temps modernes* 529–30 (August 1990).

Villani, Arnaud, 'La métaphysique de Deleuze' [critique of Badiou's *Deleuze*], *Futur antérieur* 43 (1998): 55–70.

Wahl, François, 'Le soustractif.' Preface. Badiou, *Conditions* (1992): 9–54.

Žižek, Slavoj, 'The Politics of Truth, or, Alain Badiou as a Reader of St Paul', in Žižek, *The Ticklish Subject.* London and New York: Verso, 1999. 127–70. [An abridged version of this essay appeared as 'Psychoanalysis in Post-Marxism: The Case of Alain Badiou', *South Atlantic Quarterly* 97:2 (Spring 1998): 235–61].

——'Political Subjectivization and its Vicissitudes', *The Ticklish Subject.* 171–243.

Index